An Old Guy's Guide to LIVING YOUNG

Bob Barnes

HARVEST HOUSE PUBLISHERS
EUGENE, OREGON

Cover illustration © Cedric Hohnstadt: www.cedricstudio.com

Cover by Dugan Design Group, Bloomington, Minnesota

AN OLD GUY'S GUIDE TO LIVING YOUNG
Copyright © 2013 by Bob Barnes
Published by Harvest House Publishers
Eugene, Oregon 97402
www.harvesthousepublishers.com

Library of Congress Cataloging-in-Publication Data
Barnes, Bob, 1933-
An old guy's guide to living young / Bob Barnes.
    pages cm
ISBN 978-0-7369-5275-0 (pbk.)
ISBN 978-0-7369-5276-7 (eBook)
1. Conduct of life. 2. Success. I. Title.
BJ1589.B37 2013
248.4—dc23

2013020200

Printed in the United States of America

13 14 15 16 17 18 19 20 21 / VP-CD / 10 9 8 7 6 5 4 3 2 1

I dedicate this book to all of you who want to make an impact on the next generation. By picking up this book, you've already affirmed that you want to continue to influence your children, your grandchildren, and the people around you. Your offspring will remember you long after you're no longer here on earth in your present form. They will think back and ask, "What would Grandpa do in this situation?"

Attitude is so important in staying young in thoughts and actions as we get older. I've been blessed with good health. I've learned to laugh often. And I've remained moderate in my behavior. At an early age I established my faith in God, and I've used His principles and the teachings of His Son, Jesus, as my lighthouse. I hope the thoughts in this book will help you draw closer to God, your family, your friends, and the next generation.

I encourage you to continue to stay informed regarding your family members' lives. You have a great classroom to teach those who follow after you.

∽

By wisdom a house is built,
And by understanding it is established;
And by knowledge the rooms are filled
With all precious and pleasant riches.

PROVERBS 24:3-4 NASB

Acknowledgments

The writer of a book gets much of the credit for creating the content, but it takes the competent staff of the publisher to make a total package of the actual end product—the book.

I would like to give credit to all of those at Harvest House Publishers who made this book possible.

There is one person in particular who deserves special recognition—Hope Lyda, my editor. Without her creativity in arranging the text and forming cohesive chapters, it wouldn't have come together as it has. Hope, thank you for your belief in and dedication to this project. I appreciate your many hours dedicated to this book. My hat is off to you for your insightful contributions.

Contents

Ace the Test of Time!

Today I face two big events in my life. I'm mentally preparing to take my driver's license renewal test for the state of California, and I'm emotionally preparing to celebrate my eightieth birthday this weekend. In both cases, I'm ready. I'm even glad to welcome the achievements of the small and big milestones they represent. To prepare for a driver's test, we know what to do: study the manual and learn the laws. But how can we prepare for our later years? Is there any grade, such as "pass" or "no pass," when it comes to the test of time?

Yes, there is! How can we make sure we'll pass? We can ace the test of time by continuing to be young at heart. Yes, there will be a time when we quit having birthdays. At that point, God will hopefully say to each of us, "Well done, good and faithful servant!" That will be the ultimate thumbs up! We get an A+, so we get to go to the head of the class.

I don't know about you, but I look forward to the day the Lord reviews my life and my heart and sees that I've worked hard to be faithful, loyal, and compassionate. Oh what a day that will be! But until that day comes, I will continue to prepare by being an old guy who lives young by staying active; loving my family; caring deeply and sharing openly with the people I encounter, especially when it comes to younger folks; and looking forward to the new adventures God has in store. I hope that's what you want to do too!

Time Is on Our Side

Time moves along quickly and takes us with it, whether we want that or not. Sometimes we turn around and barely recall all that has happened in our wake. But ready or not here we are. We have arrived at this stage in life that gives us the high calling of being "seniors." We've been fortunate to endure the ups and downs of life to arrive at this sacred throne of honor.

Many people think time is the enemy, but I say time is on our side when we live each moment with gratitude and a willingness to keep growing into the men of God we were born to be. Time is on our side when we look at the clock and, instead of mourning its forward motion, acknowledge the gift of another wonderful hour to spend with a loved one or gazing in awe at the sunset.

I want to encourage you and me to celebrate the honor of being in this place in our lives. No matter what our ages, I pray we'll glean some great lessons along this journey we're embarking on. Through inspirational stories, bits of wisdom, and some godly principles, we'll discover how we can best help those who are younger than we are.

Let's jump right in and enjoy this season. It can be the most exciting and blessed of all our seasons so far. I love the sentiment in this quote: "Today is the oldest you've been, yet the youngest you'll ever be, so enjoy it while it lasts" (author unknown).

Earning an A+

When we view our lives as gifts from God and the *way* we live our lives as gifts to those who come after us (and to God), we will ace the test of time. Even though our bodies tell us—even shout at us—"We're getting old!" we can still let those around us know we're young in heart, thought, and spirit. We can model a vibrant, open to learning, loving attitude for every person we encounter.

Will Rogers, the great American humorist, said, "Eventually you will reach a point in life when you stop lying about your age and start bragging about it." He also said, "When you are dissatisfied and would like to go back to your youth, just think about Algebra." What good reminders! Our test is not to relive and redo our younger years, complete with its trials and triumphs. No, our goal is to walk with integrity and joy through right now. God said through Moses,

> I have set before you life and death, blessings and curses. Now choose life, so that you and your children may live (Deuteronomy 30:19 NIV).

For those of us still in the first half of life, may the thoughts in this book give us encouragement to nurture and model godly character. For those of us living in the second half of life, may we continue to press on in shining splendor to please God. While we are all seeking to shine brightly as examples of living young, let us also take time to notice the bright aspects of living long—and there are many! Here are some pluses to whet a positive mindset:

- We receive senior discounts on food, lodging, and prescription drugs.

- We have less peer pressure.

- We don't have to pay a penalty when we withdraw from retirement accounts.

- We forget names, but it's okay because other people forget they even know us.

- Our old faces still reflect our loving hearts.

I hope to encourage you as we explore a wide variety of topics and special sections that include "God's 'Living Young' Wisdom" and "Your Guide to Living Young." While I'm going to draw on specifics from my life for examples, my prayer is you'll recognize much of your own journey in these pages.

At the end of each chapter, I've provided a short summary and some questions to help you think about this season of life with a fresh perspective. You can use the questions as reflections for your personal quiet time; as talking points for conversations with your wife, family, and friends; or as fodder for writing your own guide for living young. At the close of each chapter is a "PaPa Bob's Prayer" to gently ease you into spending time with the Lord. (Yep, my grandchildren call me PaPa Bob. I love it!)

God gives His people a desire to fellowship with Him and grow in Him. In unity, you and I can draw strength from each other and find even greater purposes for this important season in our lives. If you're like me, you want the love of God to flow through you and then move into the lives of those you love and care for. This is what we were made for! I'm so thankful God doesn't expect us to take achievement tests. I am pleased and happy that He allows us to pass on to our families, friends, and acquaintances the character, wisdom, and other riches we've discovered and acquired through the years.

Are you ready to dive in to this new adventure? I am!

1

Laugh Lines Are Free, but Wisdom Is Earned

Incline your ear and hear the words of the wise,
and apply your mind to my knowledge.

Proverbs 22:17

It can be quite a jolt to some of us the first time we go to our mailboxes and find envelopes addressed to us from Medicare and senior citizen organizations mixed in with the bills, notices, and various catalogs featuring active lifestyles. Even when we consider ourselves put-together individuals who recognize the value of the human life cycle, the realization that we are now eligible to be card-carrying members of the "older generation" can be a blow to our egos and our once-secure sense of identity.

Like me, I'm sure you've known people who start acting old before their time. They go from vibrant and active life participants to sideline observers all because they got a piece of mail that reminded them they weren't 40 anymore. Maybe we find ourselves doing this very thing! My friend, there is much joy in this time of life. We need to look at those laugh lines adorning our faces with appreciation! They are gifts from time spent with others and with God in His great creation. We don't want to allow ourselves to become one of the "sideliner old-timers." There's no need. As we explore perspectives, attitudes, purposes, and decisions through these chapters, we'll discover hope and joy no matter what discount cards we carry. (In fact, those cards should be celebrated. Use them and be glad for the extra consideration. Wise men know not to challenge a good deal when it comes their way.)

Wisdom Increases with Time and Experience

One of the advantages of growing older is that people perceive us as being wise. My grandson Chad refers to me, his "PaPa Bob," as being the wisest man he knows. What a compliment! My wisdom doesn't come from head knowledge as much as it comes from heart knowledge. By heart knowledge, I mean truths and insights from God's Word and from a life spent learning, hoping, praying, laughing, teaching, sharing, and gathering wisdom.

The older I become, the more I'm certain that living from the heart has huge value. Our faces and bodies change. Our family and financial situations change. But when we choose to live from our hearts and our hearts are centered in God, we are able to carry on and even celebrate no matter what unfolds around us.

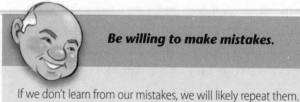

Be willing to make mistakes.

If we don't learn from our mistakes, we will likely repeat them. Don't be afraid to take bold steps even though you may encounter problems. You want to experience life's fullness and be encouraged about what events might come tomorrow.

Something I still have in common with my younger self is that I want to live a life that is meaningful to God, my family, my friends, and me. I want my decisions to be based on my belief in God and His Son, Jesus Christ. I don't want my decisions to be based on convenience, people pressure, or selfishness. The intention to live with honor has been with me for a long, long time, but the *how* of this equation has come to me gradually through the wisdom I've gleaned and gathered. (I was and still am a teacher, so I can't help myself when it comes to asking "how" questions.) Thankfully, God continues to shape me by working with my blunders, my personality traits, my quirks, and the trials I face that help me grow. I love that He is with me during every sweet moment of success and joy too.

One of the benefits of standing here, in this place beyond midlife, is being able to look back and see how God has been faithful. We can rest in the security of His presence and patience because we've experienced Him firsthand over and over. We didn't have as much time and history with God when we were younger. When I was in my thirties and raising a young family with my dear wife, Emilie, I was working in the California school system and making decisions that benefited students and teachers alike. I had great faith, but I didn't have the long journey with God to look back on, to draw strength from, and to rejoice in. In many ways, I was just beginning to understand what it means to "live in faith" and to experience the joy and peace Jesus gives freely to all who choose to believe in Him.

When We Don't Punch a Time Clock

Many people who are of retirement age are still working because of preference, passion, or finances. Whether we're fully retired or are still spending time in the land of paychecks, this time of life presents new ways to view work and vocation. Again, wisdom gained from experience and time sheds light on every part of our lives, including the efforts of our hearts and hands.

In the very beginning, God placed Adam in a beautiful garden and told him to work and take care of all the plants. In chapter one of Genesis, we read how "God created mankind in his own image…male and female" (verse 27). After their creation, He blessed them and said to them, "Be fruitful and increase in number; fill the earth and subdue it. Rule over the fish in the sea and the birds in the sky and over every living creature that moves on the ground" (verse 28).

"The LORD God took the man and put him in the Garden of Eden to work it and take care of it" (2:15). Eden was not a retail shop, a factory, or a specific place of employment, but work was part of the responsibility God bestowed on mankind in that place of origin. The same is true for our lives in the garden of our latter years. Even if we no longer punch a time clock, we still work with God to create meaning and purpose in our lives. We are blessed with the responsibility of living with intention and faith. And we are to be good stewards in everything we do.

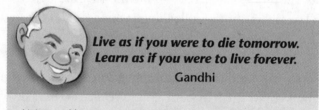

Live as if you were to die tomorrow.
Learn as if you were to live forever.
Gandhi

Living and learning are what make life so meaningful. Keep expanding your mind, and you will find more pleasure in living.

Who Are We Pleasing?

Early artisans, painters, and craftsmen sought to do work that would be pleasing to God. Their work had an excellence about it because it was created to please Him. Their efforts were a reflection of how they saw God in their lives. The culture today leans the opposite way. Work is often done with attitudes of frustration, disappointment, and halfheartedness. There is no gratitude or praise to be seen in the efforts or the results.

So who are we trying to please? Whether we're retired during this season or are still actively working in business, we're faced with this question and the call to live out the answer. When we get up in the morning and step into the day, are we aiming to please God or man? God or self? Self or others? Does God smile when He sees our work? Our work should bring Him pleasure!

> Whatever you do, whether in word or deed, do it all in the name of the Lord Jesus, giving thanks to God the Father through him…Whatever you do, work at it with all your heart, as working for the Lord, not for human masters, since you know that you will receive an inheritance from the Lord as a reward. It is the Lord Christ you are serving (Colossians 3:17,23-24).

I've had to wipe the sweat off my brow with a handkerchief and ask myself as I lean over a shovel, "Why is work so hard?" Many of us find ourselves in seasons of life when we also ask, "Why is the labor of living so hard?" Many challenges and disappointments drive us into God's waiting arms. When life is hard, it doesn't mean we aren't on the path of faith or walking with God. Our labor might be exactly what draws us back to secure God's strength. Paul writes to the church at Ephesus, "We are God's handiwork, created in Christ Jesus to do good works, which God prepared in advance for us to do" (Ephesians 2:10). When we believe God has prepared in advance work for us to do during this season of life, we will awaken with a stronger sense of purpose. This isn't a season of fading away—it's a time of great harvest!

God's "Living Young" Wisdom

I think some of the benefits of growing older are having opportunities and more time available to realize what the Word taught us in our youth and to put into motion the lessons Jesus taught His followers, including us. As I go back and meditate on His words recorded in Luke 10:25-37, I see the story of "The Good Samaritan" as a compelling parable.

The Story

A man was going down from Jerusalem to Jericho, when he was attacked by robbers. They stripped him of his clothes, beat him and went away, leaving him half dead. A priest happened to be going down the same road, and when he saw the man, he passed by on the other side. So too, a Levite, when he came to the place and saw him, passed by on the other side. But a Samaritan, as he traveled, came where the man was; and when he saw him, he took pity on him. He went to him and bandaged his wounds, pouring on oil and wine. Then he put the man on his own donkey, brought him to an inn and took care of him. The next day he took out two denarii and gave them to the innkeeper. "Look after him," he said, "and when I return, I will reimburse you for any extra expense you may have" (Luke 10:30-35).

This passage introduces four main characters:

- an injured man
- a priest
- a Levite man
- a Samaritan man

The priest was a legalist, a holy man of the Jewish temple in Jerusalem. He was a keeper of the hundreds of laws that are found in the Torah. He was a scholar of Jewish law. If he had chosen to help the injured man and the man died, the priest would become unclean according to Jewish law. He would have to go through a lengthy process to become ceremonially clean to enter the temple. When he didn't stop, it probably wasn't because he was a bad man. No, according to Jewish law, as a priest he was not to touch a man who might be on the verge of dying or dead unless it was an immediate family member (Leviticus 21:4; Numbers 19:11).

The Levites were the priestly line who served in the temple. So the Levite man who passed the injured or dead man was also constrained by Jewish law. He too would want to avoid becoming contaminated. Perhaps that's why he didn't cross the road to help.

The injured man on the side of the road was probably a Jewish traveler going from Jerusalem down to Jericho—a road known for bad things happening to travelers.

The Samaritans were people of mixed heritage, including some who were of Jewish and Gentile heritage. Jews did not associate with Samaritans, who were detested, considered social outcasts, and worshipped pagan gods (John 4:9,22). But on this day, a Samaritan man not only stopped to give aid to the injured traveler, but he put the man on his donkey, took him to an inn, paid the innkeeper two denarii (the equivalent of wages for two days of labor), and said he would return to pay any other expenses incurred.

Through this story, commonly called "The Good Samaritan," Jesus was answering questions posed by an expert in Jewish law. "What must I do to inherit eternal life?" the man had asked. After being told to "love your neighbor as yourself," the lawyer asked, "Who is my neighbor?" And Jesus replied with the Good Samaritan parable.

This story inspires us and teaches us to love people who are different from us. It could be a difference in nationality, color, religion, class status, and so forth. The bottom line is we are to love. We show the world we are Christians by our love.

After finishing His parable, Jesus asks the Torah scholar which of the three men was the "neighbor" of the injured man. The scholar replied, "The one who had mercy on him." Then Jesus told him, "Go and do likewise" (verse 37).

And this is our challenge too as we enter our senior years. We are to love those who are different from us and be servants to God and the people around us.

Sharing the Harvest

Emilie and I have used every opportunity to teach our grandchildren about God and creation. When they were little, they loved to use their hands to till the soil, scatter seeds in little trenches, cover the seeds with fertile soil, and help with the first watering. Who doesn't love the freedom to get dirty? It was always exciting to share the first harvest together too. Since there was always more than we needed, they got to take some home for their families. They discovered that sharing the fruits of their labor, literally and figuratively, was a great treasure. They understood, even when they were little, that they were partnering with God in the labor and in the giving and receiving.

Proverbs 13:22 says, "A good person leaves an inheritance for their children's children." As Emilie and I entered our golden years (that aren't always golden), we wanted to further develop our mindset of being servants. After all, Jesus said, "The Son of Man did not come to be served, but to serve, and to give his life as a ransom for many" (Matthew 20:28).

It takes unselfish love to give to others what we feel is important in life. Many grandparents have said to me, "I've raised my children. Now let *them* raise their children" or "I've put in my years of labor, now let others do the work." There's a lot of truth in that. There needs to be a healthy balance. But we don't want to be a graying population that takes the easy way out and says, "I've met my obligation. Now it is time to travel and have fun. The other things are not my responsibility." If you see your whole life as an adventure in giving, receiving, serving, growing, and learning, you will approach these latter years with a more helpful and hopeful perspective.

Several years ago Emilie and I were challenged to have a trust, will, and advance directives drawn up by our attorney. As we were deciding how our estate would be divided, the Proverbs 13:22 verse I just quoted challenged us to leave part of our worldly possessions to our children and our five grandchildren. Not only were they listed and included for specific inheritances, but we also set up an account (California Gift to Minors) with our stockbroker. For each birthday and at Christmastime, we make contributions to their bank accounts. Through this decision, we give each child a plot of our garden in a way. They will discover what it means to reap a good harvest because someone planted, and hopefully they'll discover that sharing with others from their own garden plot's harvest is one of the greatest joys in life.

Do you see what I'm getting at? This stage of life is its own garden. We stand like Adam did—vulnerable and in need of God for every provision. In our lives, Emilie and I are growing some of our longtime favorite interests, and we're investing in planting new crops too. Wisdom is what we plant in the soil of our extended family members' lives. We tend to its growth and harvest in joy as we watch it grow throughout our days—all of our days. We're so grateful for these years that are so rich with experiences and abundant wisdom to share so others can also discover the verdant gardens of faith, purpose, and service.

▓▓▓ YOUR GUIDE TO LIVING YOUNG ▓▓▓

When life becomes too hectic, when I'm feeling constantly rushed, there is an inner disturbance that prevents me from making well-thought-out decisions. My personal growth grinds to a halt. My prayer is, "Father God, let me be more aware of the feelings of my heart. Let me gain my wisdom from Your precious Word. Keep me on track, and help me separate Your thoughts from the world's thoughts." Do you experience times like that? Here are some questions to help you consider your life and see if there are changes you'd like to make.

1. How do you want to live your life? Act upon your
    answer today. In fact, I encourage you to revisit this
    question during a few of your quiet times with the
    Lord. Journal, pray, or just sit and ponder what you

want your life to look like, accomplish, and mean. Your current priorities will become very clear, and you can compare them to the priorities God sets for you.

2. What views of this senior season presented in this chapter helped you look at this time differently?

3. As you explore ways to live during this time of "life with youthful purpose and wisdom," what are you most worried about or excited about?

4. How has the harvest of others helped you? Write down or think about a specific event or time of life when a family member or another person made a difference in your life by sharing from his or her harvest.

5. What is your hope for your personal time of harvesting?

6. What can you do to feel more connected to God and His creation?

PaPa Bob's Prayer

Father God, how should I live my life? I want my faith in You to guide my decisions. I want to be calm and think clearly in every situation so I can follow Your priorities for my life. Guide me to invest in Your wisdom so I can share it with my family and future generations. I want to please You, Lord. I don't want to worry about what others think. I will follow whatever You want me to do to help a family member, friend, or stranger in need. Show me how to live out my faith in You with compassion and conviction. Amen.

2

A Good Man Loves Thanksgiving— Unless He's a Turkey

If we have food and covering, with these we shall be content.

1 Timothy 6:8

Thanksgiving isn't just for November anymore. It's a year-round mindset for men of all ages. For those of us who have enjoyed our share of turkey breast and cranberry sauce, we've been stuffed enough to spend the rest of our days grateful for the bounty of abundant times...and also for the lean times that drew us closer to our God. So unless you're the turkey to be served at dinner, the spirit of Thanksgiving should add kick to your step and spark to your efforts throughout every day. In fact, each morning when you get up is a reason to be thankful!

Emilie and I have met many amazing people through our years of being together, the years of our ministry, and the years spent in hospitals during Emilie's long battle against cancer. We've found that there are many hurting and angry people who struggle to embrace the concept of maintaining a thankful heart. We can spot these people by their countenances. They often have furrowed brows and grim mouths. They seem to have forgotten there are things to be thankful for in every situation.

If we find ourselves forgetting to be thankful or being so immersed in a painful time that we can't imagine being joyful and thankful again, we can let the information in this chapter boost our morale. We're going to look at how a change of attitude can alter more than just one day's mood. It can change how we see the world and how we interact with the people who share it with us. God transforms us, and when we partner with Him, we'll experience life in ways that exceed our expectations and provide great hope for the future.

Watch Out for That Speck

Jesus was a carpenter by trade. He knew the difference between a speck of sawdust and a log. He knew a speck was a small wood shaving while a log was large enough to be sawed into planks. So when we read Luke 6:41, we can be sure He understood the considerable challenge He was presenting. Jesus asked, "Why do you look at the speck in your brother's eye, but do not perceive the plank in your own eye?" (NKJV). What did He mean? Oftentimes we want to correct a small concern or flaw we see in someone else's life even though we're carrying around a much bigger problem. It seems like we want to live in a perfect world. In reality, what we really want is to help others be perfect (according to our definition), while we continue on, blissfully unaware of our own flaws. It doesn't work that way.

Don't cry because it's over; smile because it was.

Learn to enjoy the moment. There will always be the birth of a dream and, eventually, the death of a dream. Enjoy the entire time—from beginning to end. The journey is often more fun and fulfilling than actually reaching the final destination.

Because we want others to be flawless, and they want the same from us, I've noticed that compliments are becoming rare. Nothing seems to be good enough. "It was okay, but it was too sweet." "The noise was too loud." "The traffic was too heavy." "That color didn't look good on you." "It could've been better." Emilie and I have acquaintances who were asked by the manager in a certain restaurant not to come back. These friends were overly critical of the restaurant staff. They wouldn't quit complaining.

In our beach community in California, there are two activist groups who are trying to make the city council consider changing some laws in our area: 1) eliminate leaf blowers used by homeowners and gardeners, and 2) allow no more fires, even within fire rings, on the beach. They say the blowers make too much noise and the fires produce too much smoke. Both groups have received a lot of press and caused a significant division of opinion in our city.

In my opinion, that sort of divisiveness happens when we focus on the speck in another person's eye or the burning log on someone else's beach and ignore the bigger issues that surround us. Our view becomes smudged when we strain to see the problems in other people's actions rather than looking at trouble closer to home...in our own hearts and actions.

While Emilie was going through cancer treatment in the beautiful city of Seattle, Washington, we lived at a long-stay hotel near the treatment center. We were on the shores of Lake Union and had a lovely western view. We saw some of the prettiest sunsets at eventide. There was an abundance of boats of all sizes and shapes passing by. After a few weeks, I noticed the view wasn't quite as clear as it was when we first moved in. The lovely homes on the bluff across the way didn't seem as close or as impressive as they did at the beginning of our stay. I considered going to an eye doctor to see if my vision had changed.

One day as I was reflecting on this situation, Emilie, with her household wisdom, asked, "Do you think the windows need to be washed?" It so happened that within the next two days our hotel floor's windows were washed. And guess what? I discovered I didn't need to see the eye doctor! The view and sunsets were once again pristine and beautiful.

How often we overlook our failures and sins while being critical of people in similar situations. Are we looking through the smudges of our own lives to criticize others? We need to look at the logs in our own eyes before we try to take the sawdust specks out of the eyes of other people. When we consider how much freedom we have and the joys we experience, we realize what a waste it is to use our energy not to express gratitude but to give voice to grievances. Even in the midst of horrible situations and brutal conditions, we can find something to be grateful for. Consider these thoughts from a survivor of one of the horrific concentration camps the Germans operated during WWII. Viktor Frankl recalls:

> We who lived in concentration camps can remember the men who walked through the huts comforting others, giving away their last piece of bread. They may have been few in number, but they offer sufficient proof that everything can be taken away from a man but one thing: the last of the human freedoms—to choose one's attitude in any given set of circumstances, to choose one's own way.

Who Do You Want to Be Like?

We often need to clean the windows of our perspective so we can see the good more clearly. Different stages of our lives can also cause us to see our family members in a different light or even to be seen by them in a different light. For example, I'm amazed at how the images of fathers have changed over my lifetime. I can remember with loving pride when my son, Brad, said as a little boy, "I want to be just like you, Dad." Then a few years later, this child who once looked up to me started questioning everything I did. He viewed my advice as irrelevant to his life. That happens in the best of father/child relationships. Often, when the young person grows into adulthood, he or she realizes again that Dad does have some wisdom worth heeding. And after the person becomes a parent, a new appreciation sets in for all his father went through while raising him.

If you're facing a similar pattern with your grandkids right now, let me be an encouragement to you. This phase will soon pass! And we grandparents will once again become popular. We need to continue to love and support our grandchildren through prayer until they come back around. And our grandchildren often especially need our love and support during those times when they seem to least deserve it. They will eventually grow wise and return to us with their questions about life. One of our jobs as grandparents is to continue to be available to them no matter what so they'll know they can always come to us.

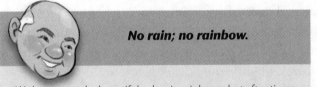

No rain; no rainbow.

We love to see the beautiful colors in rainbows, but oftentimes we forget it has to rain first. Even if we don't like the timing of the rain, we surely love to witness the beautiful results.

So let's remember to thank God along the way for our grandchildren. And if we look closely, I'm sure we'll discover these precious children can be constant sources of learning opportunities for us...about human nature, the current culture, new innovations, newfangled inventions, and the world around us. Emilie and I are blessed with five wonderful grandchildren and a great-granddaughter who are responsible for helping us gain more wisdom each passing year.

Our grandson Chad experienced a stage while growing up when he was either up or down. There was no halfway point for him. His highs were as extreme as his lows. "Attitude" was his saint and his demon. Over the years his biggest enemy was his attitude. One year for his birthday, Emilie and I gave him a coffee mug with "ATTITUDE" printed in bold letters. He placed it on the shelf over his bed so that each day when he woke up, his eyes and brain would spot this cup and take in the message. The word was a reminder that he was in charge of choosing which attitude he'd embrace for the day.

I believe choosing our attitude is one of the most significant decisions we make on a daily basis. The attitude I choose either keeps me on a positive path or hinders my progress and steers me toward grumpiness, negativity, and probably a round or two of pointing out the specks in people's eyes. When my attitude is in line with God's standards and principles, however, nothing can stop me from accomplishing my dreams. Even when I'm in a deep and dark valley, no situation is too great for me to handle because I know God is by my side. Yes, we choose our attitudes, and God provides plenty of reasons why we can focus our perspective toward gratitude and thanksgiving.

As time and experience gives us opportunities to improve on our areas of weaknesses, our growing children and grandchildren get the same. Chad no longer has to look at that mug every morning as a reminder. Maturity has helped him overcome his tendency toward holding a negative attitude. He's a discerning young man who seeks to have a good attitude in relation to family, friends, work, and decisions that need to be made. He has learned to make good choices, and his positive attitude shows.

By noticing the changes in Chad, I was also challenged to notice changes—or lack of changes—in my own journey. Thankfully, I'm still growing and learning. I can make choices that stunt those activities, but there is not an age we reach when we're expected to have "arrived" and no longer need to grow. We weren't created to stagnate. We were created to grow! And through Christ, we want to constantly work toward becoming more godly men and developing into richer, more mature versions of ourselves.

If you and I look back on the past few years and think nothing has changed, it might be time to get ourselves mugs with the word "ATTITUDE" scrawled across them. Besides, who wouldn't benefit from a daily reminder to be more grateful?

GOD'S "LIVING YOUNG" WISDOM

The United States of America has a debt load that is in the trillions—really an incomprehensible number for most of us. We look at the numbers and wonder what the solution is. Many of us have experienced personal debt or watched people we know crumble under the weight of huge medical costs, high mortgage payments, and monthly credit card bills that devastate financial stability and family life. We sit back, look around at all we have, and ask, "When is enough…enough?"

As recorded in the book of Mark, the Pharisees tried to trick Jesus with a question on "drawing a line in the sand," in this instance relating specifically to taxes. "Is it lawful to pay a poll-tax to Caesar, or not?" (12:14 NASB). They were really asking, "Is it in accordance with the Torah, our sacred law, to pay taxes to Caesar?" The poll-tax was imposed by Rome on every Jew. The burning question in the minds of many Jews of that day was "If God gave the land of Israel to us, and if God meant us to live here, and if He receives our sacrifices and offerings in acknowledgement of His relationship to us, why should we pay tribute to any other power—king, god, or person?" In answering their question, if Jesus said they should pay the tax, He could then be charged with disloyalty to the law of Judaism. If Jesus said not to pay the tax, the Jewish leaders could denounce Him to the Romans.[1]

So they asked Jesus, "Shall we pay or shall we not pay?" (verse 15). Jesus knew it was a trick. He asked them to bring Him a denarius to look at. After they did, Jesus asked, "Whose likeness and inscription is this?" They quickly replied, "Caesar's." Then Jesus gave His wise reply, "Render to Caesar the things that are Caesar's, and to God the things that are God's" (verse 17). Needless to say, the questioners were amazed by Jesus' wisdom.

Mark goes on to tell of a poor lady who gave to the temple treasury two copper coins. Jesus, while in the temple, had observed how people were giving to the treasury—a lot of people were giving large sums of money, but this one woman had put in only two coins that amounted to a cent. After making this observation, Jesus called His disciples together and told them what He'd seen. Then He said, "Truly I say to you, this poor widow put in more than all the contributors to the treasury; for they all put in out of their surplus, but she, out of her poverty, put in all she owned, all she had to live on" (Mark 12:43-44).

Jesus respected the love and devotion this poor lady gave to God. She knew God would take care of her needs. I believe this is gratitude in its purest form. When we give even though we have little, we are showing faith in God's faithfulness. Such trust honors our Lord and Savior.

A Strong, Gentle Man

Women love to be in the presence of a manly man. Such a man makes her feel feminine, self-confident, and relaxed. We don't have to be macho, have tattoos, ride gnarly motorcycles, or have sculpted muscles. Just as God values the worthiness of a man's heart, a woman loves what's inside a man more than what's outside. A godly woman prizes his leadership, steadfastness, dependability, good character, and willingness to let God do the directing.

A man who is strong when he has to be while maintaining a gentle spirit has tranquility and models the fruit of the Spirit to the people around him. These qualities, a direct result of his relationship with God, are "love, joy, peace, patience, kindness, goodness, faithfulness, gentleness, self-control" (Galatians 5:22-23). When a man is right with God, he doesn't feel any need to prove himself. If he is confident in himself and aware of his God-given strengths, he doesn't feel compelled to use his strength to control people. He enjoys an inner contentment that is based on his relationship with Jesus, not on earthly accomplishments, status, bank account, title, authority, power, or people's opinions.

Are we this kind of man? Or are we afraid to be gentle because others might consider us unmanly? Godliness isn't about being macho or all powerful. If anything, godliness is about service and humility. This is *true* strength—strength in the Lord and, in my opinion, great strength of character. A man who can be humble and gentle is a man who has confidence far beyond what the world sells to men in the form of bravado.

The husband who fails to give his wife due consideration can hardly pray sincerely with her. He must have a clear conscience before he can approach his wife for truly mutual prayer. Godly women love men who provide spiritual leadership and make time available to pray together.

If you want to pray with your wife but have never taken the initiative to do so, why not begin today?

Celebrate Contentment

Paul wrote to the church in Philippi, "I have learned to be content in whatever circumstances I am. I know how to get along with humble means, and I also know how to live in prosperity; in any and every circumstance I have learned the secret of being filled and going hungry, both of having abundance and suffering need" (Philippians 4:11-12).

The Scriptures teach us to be satisfied. If we are content with what we have, we find cause to celebrate the small and the big moments. We celebrate when we rejoice in God's creation and work to make our lives more productive and fulfilling. We celebrate when we spend time interacting with our families. We celebrate through our willingness to share, to love, to provide, to grow. And we celebrate by opening our hearts to the Lord and letting the Holy Spirit fill our lives with love and abundance.

Celebrating life leads to even more gratitude. The more grateful we are for God's care and provision, the more willing we are to release our hold on money and possessions. The more we're willing to release, the more we freely give to help others, which helps us better understand and appreciate God's freely given grace and mercy. Rejoice in the Lord *always* (Philippians 4:4)! The spirit of celebration can be found in little moments of grace as well as in rambunctious revelry. We discover joy when we experience deep satisfaction in accomplishing any humble task done for God's glory. Our happiness grows through an understanding, private glance with someone just as much as it does interacting with a group of people at a large gala.

We celebrate because our lives overflow with God's love and the many blessings He gives to us.

YOUR GUIDE TO LIVING YOUNG

1. When you notice what you're learning from your wife, your kids, your grandkids, your friends, and from God's Word, don't forget to pay attention to what you also learned during your growing-up years. If your dad is still alive, why not call or write him and tell him how much you appreciated his wisdom over the years? If he is no longer with you, write him a letter as if he were still alive. Thank him for being your dad.

2. Remembering your journey as a boy can help you see the ways you've changed and the ways you are still the same. Both observations provide comfort and assurance because they reveal that God made you

uniquely you. He calls you to become more grounded in your faith by honing your values and sharing them. May you never consider yourself done growing!

3. What reminds you to be grateful each day? Consider getting yourself a special "ATTITUDE" mug or maybe a screensaver that presents a Scripture or words of encouragement for your eyes and mind to take in every morning. We all need reminders to stay upbeat.

4. What is the log in your eye that you need to deal with?

5. Who do you need to show grace to right now?

6. What opportunities will you have today to extend genuine compliments to people?

7. Who do you want to be like and why?

PaPa Bob's Prayer

God, hold me back from looking for the speck in another person's eye when I have so much to work on in my own life. Remind me to be humble and grateful for the good and bad times, for the highs and lows of being a man, a husband, a parent, a grandparent, and an ever-growing child of Yours.

Help me seek Your wisdom with a grateful, open heart so that I can learn from You. Keep me open to wisdom from those You place in my life. Today I'm very thankful for the lessons I've learned from my parents and for how my family and friends teach me what it means to be a thankful man instead of just another aging turkey. Amen.

❧ A Legacy Moment ❧

by *Brad Barnes* (Bob's son)

How Dad Models Living Young

- When I try to get a jump on my dad and show up 10 minutes early for our 7 o'clock breakfast, he's already there. I'd have to get up very early to match his energy.

- At special occasions, such as weddings, Dad is always the first one there to help and the last one to leave. As I take off, I look over and he's still holding court with the hosts and guests.

- Several years ago I moved my family into a new home. Dad was waiting in my driveway wondering why the moving company was late. He might not move as many boxes as he used to, but he's always pushing the pace to get the final box unpacked. I sit down for a rest, and he's still working away!

- Dad stays young and active by supporting and attending local high school sporting events.

How Dad Inspires Me

- His dedication and commitment to God and his appetite to learn more.

- His ability to accomplish so much. He's still writing books, reading everything he can get his hands on, attending every family event, and taking great care of my mom.

- His desire tp put others before himself.

- His passionate and mighty love for our family.

Now's the Time for a Modeling Career

Now that I am old and gray, do not abandon me, O God.
Let me proclaim your power to this new generation,
your mighty miracles to all who come after me.

Psalm 71:18 NLT

Don't worry. I'm not really expecting us to start walking down runways wearing the latest fashions, although our families probably would appreciate it if we wore pants without holes in the knees. The truth is that, ready or not, now is a great time in life to model our faith in Christ and ways to live for Him. Our modeling career has been in the works for some time, and now we're front and center...well-worn pants and all.

People around us are paying attention to how we live out our beliefs and exhibit concern for others. If we're throwing up our hands in this season of life, saying, "I guess my days of being influential are over," then we have another lesson or two coming our way. Right now, right this moment, is a wonderful point in our time line to show others the heart, and hands, and love of Jesus.

Have you ever felt you've been in the presence of people with a special relationship with God? They seem to radiate the love God would if He were physically standing in the room. When we learn of their faith, it brings us to a fuller appreciation of who they are and what kind of people they are. In today's politically correct climate, we are often hesitant to mention God because we don't want to be too forward and put people in an uncomfortable situation. Sometimes, however, there is something about their demeanor that gives us an indication they are believers in Jesus. There's something upbeat about how they carry themselves. Those kind of people can make a huge difference in someone's life within a matter of minutes. And that is the kind of person we can be during this season of our lives.

Do people around us know we're followers of Jesus? Do our friends, neighbors, and people at work know from our presence and behavior that we have a personal love relationship with Him? While Emilie was battling cancer as a patient at the University of Washington Medical Hospital (located on campus adjacent to Lake Washington), we found ourselves talking frequently with one of the nurses. We expressed how our faith in Jesus was the reason for our optimism and hope. Many times she'd share with us about her life and get teary eyed. We listened with compassion. One late-afternoon at a shift change and the beginning of four days off, this nurse came into our room to say goodbye because she knew Emilie would be switching to outpatient status. As she came into the room she said, "I don't know why I'm attracted to you both, but you have something magnetic that most patients don't have. I don't know what it is, but I like being around you."

Without hesitation Emilie responded, "What you are seeing in us is Jesus!" After a bit more conversation, the young nurse exited the room, went down the elevator, got on her bicycle (a lot of people travel to and from work on their bikes in Seattle), and rode off for her break knowing she'd been with "companions of Jesus"!

We believers are the "salt of the earth," seasoning the world around us with Jesus' love and grace (Matthew 5:13). People around us should sense that Jesus has impacted our lives and know we draw our wisdom from His Word, the Bible. We are to be different from the people in the world who don't follow Jesus. What did the nurse see in Emilie and me that she found so attractive?

- We were kind.
- We listened to her life story with care and compassion.
- We shared our faith and the Scriptures that gave us hope for healing and for life.
- We exhibited a sweet, respectful spirit toward her, including saying "thank you" and "please."
- We shared our story of love for each other as a husband and wife who had been married for 45 years and were still delighted and excited about being together. We attributed the success of our marriage to being followers of Jesus, growing in our knowledge of Him and His Word.
- We shared Jesus gently and when appropriate.

Not every person we meet will be attracted to us because we love Jesus. But the ones who are will be affected for the rest of their lives because we've chosen to reveal our personal relationship with our Lord and Savior, Jesus Christ. As men of God, let's reach out and touch someone's life today in Jesus' name. Let's pray that after we have such an encounter, the person will know he or she has been with someone who has been with Jesus (Acts 4:13).

Imitation is the sincerest form of flattery.

When others copy you, receive it as a compliment. They are letting you know they are inspired by your life. What you do is something they want to do too.

Passing the Baton of Belief

A prudent person will have a will made up stating how he wants his wealth dispersed. Financial planners play a large role in helping a person decide how to word the document so his estate isn't eaten up by taxes. Have you ever thought about how you can pass on your belief in Jesus to the next generation? We need to pass on a few basic truths to encourage, guide, and support those who follow after us. Our children, grandchildren, great-grandchildren, and others who encounter us during our senior years will learn more by watching us than by hearing us. Actions are much more powerful than words. Today our generation is in the lead, so we need to treat our role with honor and responsibility.

When we watch a relay race, we're witnessing exactly what needs to happen in our lives. As soon as the runner of one lap finishes, the race isn't over. That runner carefully and knowingly passes the baton to the next runner. If the runner for the first lap stopped short of this task, his team would lose. He needs to pass the baton on. We need to do the same when it comes to God's truths. Here are four inspirations for sharing our faith:

- *Affirm that the Lord is God.* When the Lord is our one true God, we're excited to share this truth with our grandkids and others. We want to live for Jesus and reveal our security in a sovereign God. Each time we share how God is working in our lives, we may be inspiring another person to examine how God is working in his or her life. Each time we give God credit for our successes and blessings, we invite others to give God credit for His power at work in and through them.

- *Love the Lord with whole hearts.* We don't want to hold back from giving any part of our hearts and lives to God. We are living examples of sold-out-for-God faith when we freely give the details and needs of our lives to His care. This encourages others to do the same. If we've had times of resisting God's leading in the past, then we can speak openly about what we've learned since then. Everyone from a grade-school student to a retired businessman will be interested in how we've learned to love and live completely for God. The lessons we've already learned are lessons many others might be trying to make sense of right now. Let's pass on our batons of experience!

- *Teach and train our children and the next generation.* If we think we don't have something to offer younger generations, we've forgotten the impact mentors and role models had on us. Unfortunately, some people don't have examples of godliness in their homes, and that's where we can help. No matter how we found the people who became our teachers and trainers, we benefited from their experiences and their demonstrations of God's power in action. We need to go and do the same for others. When we invest our time and energy this way, we're giving the greatest gift we can— knowledge of our Lord and Savior, Jesus Christ. That is incredibly valuable! One conversation at the right time might be the spark of hope God wants to use to lead that neighbor kid, that acquaintance, that lawn guy in the right direction. Our obedience can help change history!

- *Build a firm foundation.* Even if we've never put together a bookcase, we're builders. Every day we have opportunities to choose tools from our toolbox and use them to shape a conversation, strengthen the foundation of a relationship, or reframe a situation so God's light comes in. Our tools include our unique personal experiences, our stories, our memories, our trials, our

successes, our knowledge, and our personalities. God
is the Master builder, Architect, and Designer, and He
gives us the privilege of partnering with Him to lay a
spiritual foundation in people's lives.

As we daily live out God's principles found in His Word, others
will notice. Many times they'll ask us questions about why we live
a certain way or how we can treat others with such compassion.
The psalmist tells us not to hide God's truths from our children.
We're to tell the next generation about our Lord—about His power,
His love, and His mighty works (Psalm 78). We are commanded
to teach God's truths to our children so they will live by them
and teach them to the next generation. That way God's truths are
handed down from generation to generation.

> We will not hide these truths from our children;
>   we will tell the next generation
> about the glorious deeds of the LORD,
>   about his power and his mighty wonders.
> For he issued his laws to Jacob;
>   he gave his instructions to Israel.
> He commanded our ancestors
>   to teach them to their children,
> so the next generation might know them—
>   even the children not yet born—
>   and they in turn will teach their own children
> (Psalm 78:4-6 NLT).

GOD'S "LIVING YOUNG" WISDOM

One day God grabbed Moses' attention by causing a bush to
burst into flames but not burn up. When Moses approached, God
told him to go to the Egyptian pharaoh to tell him to free the Isra-
elite slaves. Moses said, "Who am I, that I should go to Pharaoh,

and that I should bring the sons of Israel out of Egypt?" (Exodus 3:11).

God replied, "Certainly I will be with you, and this shall be the sign to you that it is I who have sent you: when you have brought the people out of Egypt, you shall worship God at this mountain" (verse 12).

Moses then asked what he was to say when he went to the sons of Israel to tell them God's message. When they ask me what Your name is, what do I tell them?

And God said to Moses, " 'I AM WHO I AM'; and He said, 'Thus you shall say to the sons of Israel, "I AM has sent me to you" ' " (verse 14).

This term "I AM WHO I AM" is the meaning of the name *Yahweh*: "I am the One who is." Abbreviated to "YHWH," the name is pronounced "*Yah-weh*." This is the most significant name for God in the Old Testament. The Israelites were so fearful of dishonoring God that they didn't even want to write His complete name down.

God was telling Moses and His people that He was the One and only God. He was the Creator of the universe. He was to be lifted up and glorified.

So Moses did as God said to. He went to the Israelites and appeared before Pharaoh until the Egyptian pharaoh released the Israelites from slavery. (There's a lot more to this fascinating story! I encourage you to read Exodus 3–15).

Later on God gave Moses the Ten Commandments to give to the Israelites (Exodus 20). Notice these were not suggestions they should consider. No, they were commandments to be followed by everyone who believed in Him. God was very firm when He stated, "I am the LORD your God," and then gave the commandments, beginning with these three:

- You shall have no other gods before Me (verse 3).

- You shall not make for yourselves an idol, or any

likeness of what is in heaven above or on earth beneath
or in the water (verse 4).

- You shall not worship them or serve them for I, the
LORD your God, am a jealous God (verse 5).

God was establishing Himself as the only God to be worshipped. Are you thinking, "I don't have any gods before the one true God." In reality, you and I put many things before God when it comes to our day-to-day lives. We do this through the choices we make that put things such as money, how we spend our time, and other priorities ahead of God. Anything that takes our eyes off the Lord God can become a mini god to us.

So again I ask, do the people around us know we are "companions of God"? Every day are we giving witness to how mighty God is? Truthfully, we have been witnesses to and about our God from the very first minute we became believers! Whatever we say and whatever we do should glorify God's holy name. We are to show the world who He is. We, the people of God, need to live worthy lives so the people around us will know who *Yahweh* is and want to know Him even more. God's Word says people will know we are followers of Jesus Christ by our love (John 13:35).

Praise Pays Dividends

Ken Blanchard, a top management consultant said, "There is no doubt in my mind that the key to developing people and helping them reach their peak performance is to catch them doing things right and then recognizing their accomplishments with a pat on the back. This concept is true for managers, teachers, parents, spouses, and friends. Accentuating the positive is how effective relationships are built."[1]

When Emilie and I had five young grandchildren, we were shopping and came across bright-red stickers at a store that read, "I was caught being good!" We were excited to try these stickers as a tool of encouragement for the kids. We were always in search of ways to inspire them to do more acts of kindness on their own. So we bought a stash of those stickers and gave them a try. We knew the idea of positive reinforcement would work well with Christine because she was a girl and the stickers had teddy bears on them. We weren't sure if the boys would wear those stickers though. To our amazement, they thought it was great. They would prance around with their chests puffed up like roosters showing off for hens.

We added a little twist to the system by making each child a 8½" x 11" sheet of paper so at the end of the day they could place their earned stickers on it for safekeeping. When the sheet was full they could turn them in and Grammy and PaPa would give them 10 cents for each sticker. (We eventually upped the refund to 25 cents a sticker.) What a motivation this turned out to be for them! They couldn't resist discovering "good" behaviors. They looked for things so they could be "caught being good."

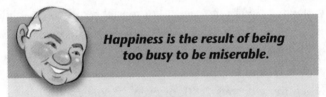

Happiness is the result of being too busy to be miserable.

An idle mind gets you into trouble. A complainer in life needs to get a life. When a person serves another person or cause, he or she finds this time in life to be the happiest time, period. Try serving rather than being served.

The value of praise to increase productivity can't be overestimated. There is no cost in giving someone a pat on the back or a sincere comment of "well done." The results are always positive.

Unfortunately, for many parents and employers, praising others doesn't come easily. A good many people make mental notes of jobs well done. Sadly, too few stop and take the time to say, "You're doing a great job," or "Thank you for your help," or "You're a very special person."

I'm Special Because...

One evening when our grandson Chad was seven, he was helping us set the dinner table. When the grandchildren come over, our tradition is to honor someone at the table with a red plate that has "You Are Special Today" written on it, even when there isn't a birthday, anniversary, or other special occasion. So I asked Chad, "Who should we honor today with our special plate?"

Chad replied, "How about *me*?"

"Yes, Chad, you are special," I answered. "It's your day."

He was so proud as we all sat around the table and said the blessing. Then Chad said, "I think it would be very nice if everyone around the table would tell me why they think I'm special." Emilie and I got a chuckle out of that, but we thought it was a good idea, so we did it. After we were all through, Chad said, "Now I want to tell you why I think I'm special. I'm special because I'm a child of God!" Chad was so right on. God knew each of us before we were born. He knit us together in our mothers' wombs. We are wonderfully made (Psalm 139:13-14).

When my wife was 7, 10, or even 22, she couldn't have told anyone why she was special. Why? One reason is because she didn't have a father who showed her or told her how special she was. When she was young, she didn't know she was a child of God. Instead, she was a shy, scared child of an alcoholic father who would go into rages, swearing and throwing things. She was afraid to say or do something because it might turn out to be wrong and set him off, so she pulled back from expressing herself. Her self-image wasn't very good. But the day came when she read Psalm 139, and her heart came alive with the realization that she too is special because she was created by the God of the universe who loves her. Like the psalmist, Emilie now says, "I praise you [God] because I am fearfully and wonderfully made; your works are wonderful, I know that full well" (Psalm 139:14 NIV).

I, on the other hand, had role models of faith around me when I was young. My family members helped me rest in the assurance that I was special and loved. How about you? When did you have an understanding of how special and loved you are? Are you letting the younger generation know about the greatness and specialness of being part of the family of God?

I am wonderfully made and so are you. We were each uniquely made as God knit us together in our mother's womb. Psalm 139:16 says, "All the days ordained for me were written in your book [of life] before one of them came to be." We have all been given unique qualities, talents, and gifts.

Yes, my friend, you were made by God. You are His child. He loves you more than any earthly father could possibly love you. Because He is your heavenly Father, your Almighty God, He cares for you even when you don't care for yourself. You are His child even when you feel far from Him. Your heavenly Father never moves away from you. When you feel a distance between you and God, it's you who has moved away from Him. And if that's the case, He's eagerly waiting for you to draw near to Him again.

I encourage you today to draw near to Him—as close as you possibly can. Today is your day! You are special today and every day. Like Chad said, you too are "a child of God!"

We Are Molders of Clay

When our son, Brad, was in elementary school, the teacher asked the class to shape clay into something. Brad proudly brought home a red dinosaur-type thing that was molded and shaped with his small hands. It still sits proudly on our bookshelf these many years later. Now his children view this prized exhibit of their father's beginning artistry.

Later, in high school, Brad enrolled in a ceramics class. His first pieces were a bit crooked and misshapen, but as time went on he made some pieces that were excellently crafted—vases, pots, pitchers, and so forth. Many pieces of clay that he threw on the pottery wheel, however, took a different direction than he first intended. Brad would work and work to reshape the clay, and sometimes he would have to start over, working and working to make it exactly the way he wanted it to be.

With each one of us, God has, so to speak, taken a handful of clay to make us exactly who He wants us to be. He is the Master Potter, and we are clay in His hands. As He shapes us on His potter's wheel, He works on the inside and the outside. He essentially says, "I am with you. I am the Lord of your life, and I will build within you a strong foundation based upon My Word." The Master Potter also uses the circumstances of life to shape us.

When a child dies, we lose our jobs, fire destroys our homes, finances dissolve, our marriages fall apart, or our children rebel, our Master Potter can seem very far away. We may even feel forgotten by God. Consequently, we pull away from Him because He "let us down." As time passes, God seems even more silent and distant. It seems like His work in our lives has been put on hold. But God said, "I will be with you; I will not fail you or forsake you" (Joshua 1:5). When we feel far from God, we need to remember that *He* didn't move away or put us on a shelf. We moved. He is always ready to continue molding us into the people He intends us to be.

In pottery, the clay is baked at a very high temperature to set it so the vessel hardens. Sometimes the true beauty of the clay comes out only after the firing. The fires of life can do the same for our faith and our character as long as we remain connected to God. When we go through trials, we can rest in the knowledge that the Master Potter is at work in our lives.

▇▇▇▇ YOUR GUIDE TO LIVING YOUNG ▇▇▇▇

Being young at heart involves having a heart for the young. It means living your life with genuine love and care for everyone who is a part of your experience.

There is a great peace that covers you when you realize you are special. How do you feel when you read Psalm 139:14? "I will give thanks to You [God], for I am fearfully and wonderfully made; wonderful are Your works, and my soul knows it very well."

1. What do the words "fearfully and wonderfully made" mean to you? Do you believe you are special in God's eyes? The joy of this belief is doubled every time you remind others how special they are. When you live out your faith through actions, words, efforts, labor, connections, and relationships, the Master Potter is able to shape every moment into an opportunity to model Jesus.

2. How is your modeling career these days? Are you showing Jesus to others?

3. When have you seen the light of Christ in another person? How did that impact you?

4. Are there traditions you have or want to have that will celebrate the specialness of each of your family members?

5. How can you live out your specialness during this time of your life? How will you choose to share your unique gifts and show Jesus to others?

PaPa Bob's Prayer

Father God, let me grasp this responsibility to pass on God's truths to my children and my children's children so they, in turn, can pass them on to their children. Help me expand my vision of modeling so I can step up and be a light to people beyond my immediate family.

Give me the courage to make a difference. When I go through my days and greet someone at a store or shake hands with someone at the bank, let that person see Christ in my life. Help me be a model of Your love and care to all I encounter. I want to show them You! Reveal to me the ways I can walk boldly and unwaveringly with compassion during this season of my life. Amen.

I Married a Good Woman; She Married a Work-in-Progress

You husbands in the same way, live with your wives in an understanding way.

1 Peter 3:7

Marriage takes work at any age; however, the riches of sharing our lives with our spouses is a blessing from God. I believe that most men require a greater learning curve about how to love and be supportive partners than women need. We men are encouraged to marry, raise a family, and be good and godly men—but when it comes down to *how* to do and be those things, we don't receive much training. It's "learning as we go," and the process can be slow, as some wives can attest. But if we are sincere in our desire, efforts, and prayers, we can be good husbands even as we're works in progress. Even at our age, it's rather nice to know we still have things to strive for.

People who are married live longer than unmarried individuals. When the media put this on the airwaves, the public said, "Really?" Yes, really! Research for decades has come to this conclusion. In my early days I thought that's what all boys were supposed to do—get married and raise families. That was and still is the norm.

And now I find it delightful when I see two grandparents walking on the beach arm in arm. It's the best kind of advertisement for the value of marriage. Their companionship reflects the truth that love and friendship can endure over time. In our youth-oriented culture, people often believe that love and friendship are only for the young and that older folks aren't supposed to still feel romantic.

A few years ago I had my left knee replaced, which required several weeks of physical therapy. During these sessions I got to know the lady therapist very well. We had many conversations as she was bending my leg (which caused a great deal of pain, I must say). At one stretch in a session, she wanted to know how long I'd been married. I told her 56 years. She responded, "I don't know how anyone could be married to the same person that long!" Then she wanted to know how we'd done it. That gave me the opportunity to share my faith as an active part of my marriage commitment. She said she'd never heard of such a marriage, and it certainly wasn't present within her family background.

Genesis 2:18-23 is a beautiful picture of how God created the first woman who would become Adam's friend and wife:

> Then the LORD God said, "It is not good for the man to be alone; I will make him a helper suitable for him." Out of the ground the LORD God formed every beast of the field and every bird of the sky, and brought them to the man to see what he would call them; and whatever the man called a living creature, that was its name. The man gave names to all the cattle, and to the birds of the sky, and to every beast of the field, but for Adam there was not found a helper suitable for him. So the LORD God caused a deep sleep to fall upon the man, and he slept; then He took one of his ribs and closed up the flesh at that place. The LORD God fashioned into a woman the rib which He had taken from the man, and brought her to the man. The man said, "This is now bone of my bones, and flesh of my flesh; she shall be called Woman, because she was taken out of Man."

Emilie is my wife, but she is also my friend. Through the years, our love has grown stronger, and we have become each other's *best* friend. This passage from Genesis suggests that is exactly what God intended for married couples!

One of the ways we model friendship in marriage for our children and grandchildren is by expressing affection and consideration for one another. Our family enjoys overhearing Emilie and me saying "I love you" to each other and witnessing other acts of love and kindness.

Alan Loy McGinnis, in his book *The Friendship Factor*, shared how husbands and wives can build a strong foundation:

> When we stop to think about it, husbands and wives cement their love with many ceremonies: kissing good-night, celebrating anniversaries, giving jewelry, telephoning when they are apart, bringing each other breakfast in bed, taking an evening walk together.[1]

If you and your spouse don't share rituals like these, or if you've quit sharing in these small-but-important gestures of care and tenderness, don't wait for your wife to reach out. Take the initiative and go first. If you've tried to reinstate these gestures and they weren't well received, ask God to guide and bless your efforts and then risk trying again.

Loving with Unconditional Love

I would like to tell you that my marriage has always been heavenly, but I can't because that wouldn't be real. Whenever I strayed from the instructions found in Ephesians 5:25-30, I experienced marital problems:

> Husbands, love your wives, just as Christ also loved the church and gave Himself up for her, so that He might sanctify her, having cleansed her by the washing of water with the word, that He might present to

Himself the church in all her glory, having no spot or wrinkle or any such thing; but that she would be holy and blameless. So husbands ought also to love their own wives as their own bodies. He who loves his own wife loves himself; for no one ever hated his own flesh, but nourishes and cherishes it, just as Christ also does the church, because we are members of His body.

Emilie and I have never talked about getting a divorce. We've never allowed that word into our marriage vocabulary. When I committed myself to Emilie "for richer or for poorer, in sickness and in health," I meant it. However, there were times when my pursuit of success wrongfully took priority over my growth as a Christian and godly husband. I put God on hold for several years. We didn't stop going through the motions of building a wonderful family life, but in my heart I knew I wasn't the spiritual husband and father God created me to be.

Life is too short to waste time with regret.

If you're walking with resentment or regret, you are on a dead-end street. Don't waste your life being negative. If you need to ask forgiveness, do it now. If you need to give forgiveness, do that now.

My turning point came when we moved to Newport Beach, California, and began attending Mariners Church. At that time I got involved with a group of men who challenged me to better fulfill my role as a Christian husband and father. I experienced a new awareness that my first responsibility, after serving God, is to serve my wife and then my family. I've endeavored to fulfill that responsibility ever since.

As husbands, our submissive, serving love for our wives is to be unconditional and committed to giving, not getting. The focus is to be on their hearts' desires, not ours. Consequently, I should never view my wife as an instrument of my pleasure or convenience, such as my nurse, servant, dishwasher, cook, or errand runner. I should never ask her to do something degrading or harmful in her eyes to fulfill my wishes or whims. She is my helpmate and my partner. We are a team with similar goals and desires. I am to continually love her and serve her for who she is, not what she can do for me.

What It Takes to Be a Good Husband

I heard this story once, and I thought it was a good one...

> God spoke to a certain man and said He'd noticed that this man was a very good husband so He would grant the husband one wish for being so responsible. The man thought for a moment and said, "I would like You to build me a bridge from Southern California to Hawaii." God quickly said that was a physically impossible engineering feat. "Since I can't give you that wish, you may have another one." After a moment's thought, the husband asked God, "You might help me understand my wife more." Without hesitation God replied, "Do you want a one-lane or two-lane bridge to Hawaii?"

As husbands, we are always trying to better understand our wives. The Scriptures say love has many mysteries, and this is certainly one of them. No matter how hard I try, Emilie remains a delightful mystery to me. (Well, most of the time it's delightful.) We have a saying in our relationship: "Women are weird, and men are strange." With that said, we still continue to try to understand each other better.

The Responsible Husband

Another passage of Scripture besides Ephesians 5:25-30 that has given me direction for my role as a husband is 1 Peter 3:7: "You husbands in the same way, live with your wives in an understanding way, as with someone weaker, since she is a woman; and show her honor as a fellow heir of the grace of life, so that your prayers will not be hindered." Peter is clearly stating that husbands must perform two responsibilities and, in return, will receive one specific reward.

Responsibility #1: Husbands are to live with their wives in an understanding way. The King James Version of 1 Peter 3:7 says we are to "dwell with them according to knowledge." What knowledge? The knowledge of wives and marriage, of course. We need to find out why "wives are weird and husbands are strange."

Learning to live with our wives in an understanding way is more on-the-job training than anything else. Seminars, books, and recordings are great, but there is no substitute for patient, observant, day-to-day living with our wives to expand our knowledge of them. Even after these many decades with Emilie, I'm still learning about her. The marriage relationship is always "in process."

Responsibility #2: Husbands are to grant their wives honor as fellow heirs of the grace of God. One of the ways we can honor our wives is by being respectful, courteous, and mannerly. Another way to honor them is by openly communicating our appreciation for who they are and what they do. We can express our appreciation in conversations with her and others, in notes and cards, and through special treatment such as a special dinner out or a getaway weekend.

We honor our wives by speaking favorably of them to others. Our wives are not our "old ladies." Our wives have names, and they have the important roles of being our wives and being the mothers of our children. Our respectful words about them will fulfill

Ephesians 4:29: "Let no unwholesome word proceed from your mouth, but only such a word as is good for edification according to the need of the moment, so that it will give grace to those who hear."

The Reward: Our communication with God will not be hindered. Peter described our wives as fellow heirs of the grace of life. That means that our wives are equal recipients of the gifts God has for us. Our generation's women's rights movement was thousands of years behind the times. God gave women a position of spiritual equality right from the beginning, when He created man and woman in the Garden of Eden. I know that some husbands feel threatened by their wives' spiritual growth, but my prayer over the years has been that Emilie will become the woman God wants her to be. I'm not threatened by her growth or her spiritual gifts, even in areas where she outshines me.

The honor we show our wives is like an investment, similar to the investments Emilie and I have made in stocks, bonds, mutual funds, certificates of deposit, and treasury bonds. Through the years we've watched our stocks increase in value and enjoyed the dividends that our investments have returned. Similarly, as we invest daily in our wives by honoring them in words and deeds, we will see them grow stronger in their sense of self-worth. Furthermore, we'll reap dividends in our marriages that greatly exceed our initial investment.

The apostle Peter also suggested that our relationships with our wives correlates directly to our relationship with God. If we fail to understand and honor our wives, our prayers will be hindered! If our horizontal relationship with our wives is in harmony, our vertical relationship with God will also be in harmony.

The Manager in the Home

During the 1950s, when Emilie and I were married, husband and wife roles were more clearly defined. In those days, the husband usually took care of everything outside the house, and the wife concerned herself with everything inside the house. We heard phrases like "That's not my job," "I'm not changing the diapers—that's the mother's job," and "The yard needs mowing—Dad and the boys will do it." Fortunately, Emilie and I didn't contract our marriage on that basis. I'd seen my father do many jobs around the home that were generally considered "woman's work," so I had no problems helping with the dishes, changing diapers, staying with the children while Emilie went to the market, ironing my shirts, and doing laundry occasionally.

Also during the 50s, the man of the house usually wrote the checks and controlled the purse strings. We were warned that it was almost considered "un-Christian" for the wife to pay the monthly bills. But I couldn't go along with that. I had a wife who was very good at finances. As a couple, we established a budget for our fixed expenses and decided together where to spend our money. Because Emilie was so good with numbers, I asked her to write the checks. This was difficult for her at first because she thought I needed to be responsible for our finances, but we figured it out together, and it works wonderfully for us.

Making people happy makes you happy.

When we serve other people, including our spouses, we will discover that we are at our happiest. It doesn't take much time to lighten the load for a loved one or friend each day. A smile, a hug, or an offer of help goes a long way to make others happy. When your wife is happy, then you will be happy.

Today the guidelines for managing the home have changed drastically. Gone are the days when husbands went to work and earned the money while wives stayed home to take care of the home and, eventually, the children. The working wife and mother is now a staple in the workforce. We recently met a retired man who stays home to cook delicious meals and keep house while his wife maintains a job outside the home. They love their new roles.

Not long ago, Emilie and I ran into a former coworker of mine in a grocery store. I asked about his family, and he said he'd quit his job to stay home and raise the children. His wife was so successful in her computer career and making so much more money than he could make, they decided to reverse the traditional roles. He loved his duties at home, and she loved her career much more than homemaking.

GOD'S "LIVING YOUNG" WISDOM

In his letter to the church at Ephesus, the apostle Paul gave some profound instructions on how we are to serve Christ in our various relationships. A key verse on this topic is Ephesians 5:21: "Be subject to one another in the fear of Christ." This verse really caught my eye because it comes *before* the specific instructions to wives and husbands. The first instruction to husbands and wives is to adopt a spirit of *mutual submission* to one another out of reverence for Christ.

A Christian husband and wife each have Christ living in them. To reverence Christ, we must reverence the vessels He dwells in. When we submit to one another, we are submitting to Christ. That's the only way verses 22 through 24 make sense: "Wives, be subject to your own husbands, as to the Lord. For the husband is the head of the wife, as Christ also is the head of the church, He Himself being the Savior of the body. But as the church is subject to Christ, so also the wives ought to be to their husbands in everything." Without an attitude of mutual submission, the husband becomes the big boss and the wife becomes the doormat. But the priority of mutual submission keeps the specific instructions to husbands and wives in proper perspective. Paul teaches husbands about their roles in Ephesians 5:25-30:

> Husbands, love your wives, just as Christ loved the church and gave himself up for her to make her holy, cleansing her by the washing with water through the word, and to present her to himself as a radiant church, without stain or wrinkle or any other blemish, but holy and blameless. In this same way, husbands ought to love their wives as their own bodies. He who loves his wife loves himself. After all, no one ever hated their own body, but they feed and care for their body, just as Christ does the church—for we are members of his body (NIV).

My first response to this instruction was "Oh, that's easy—as long as she promises to love me first, wash my clothes, cook great meals, and always look pretty." Then I remembered verse 21 and reminded myself that I can't act on the basis of such thoughts. Loving Emilie had to start with submitting to the Lord and to her. Once I grasped that principle, I submitted to Christ in a fresh, new way. Even though Ephesians 5:22 states that Emilie was to also be submissive to me, I knew I was subject to a higher calling—*mutual submission*. I began to realize that I was not to control or dominate Emilie. Instead, I was to humbly and sacrificially love her. I was to set aside my rights and serve her needs.

Fortunately I was raised in a family that modeled sacrificial love through kindness and good manners. So during my courtship with Emilie, I graciously opened the car door for her and assisted her with her chair when she was being seated at the dining table. I allowed her to go through doorways ahead of me and performed other kind acts I'd learned as a boy. Paul's instructions helped me see that the *motivation* for such kindness to Emilie was humble submission to Jesus who dwelled within her.

I heard a true story about a man whose wife had always wanted him to open the car door for her. Instead of complying, he would make fun of her request with remarks like "What's wrong with your own two hands—are they broken?" He refused to open the car door for her. The man's wife passed away. At her funeral, the husband preceded the pallbearers as they carried her casket to the hearse. Because the man was the first to arrive at the hearse, the funeral director asked him to open the door so the pallbearers could slide the casket inside. As the man reached for the door handle, he remembered his wife's persistent request. He sadly realized that the only time he'd fulfilled her wish was after she died.

At first glance, manners may seem to be a small area of submission; however, manners are a very practical way to show our reverence for Christ by serving our mates. What about your wife sparks your romantic interests and desire to serve her? Let her know!

Let's Not Live in Our Recliners

The greatest enemy of the successful husband and manager is passivity. At home we men tend to want to lay back and let things happen instead of stepping forward and making things happen. We need to not yield to the temptation to abandon our God-given role of leader. We must get on with the program. When we do, our wives, children, and those who witness our lives will have greater respect for us.

The biblical pattern for the husband's role in managing the home is found in 1 Corinthians 11:3: "I want you to realize that the head of every man is Christ, and the head of every woman is man, and the head of Christ is God" (NIV). The chain of command is clear: God above Christ, Christ above man, man above woman. This principle is often difficult to maintain in our culture because most people have forgotten the idea of mutual submission. They perceive this instruction to be about dominance when really it is about service—we men serving Christ and our wives. When we accept the role of responsible manager and carry it out with the heart of a servant, our families will flourish.

I am so thankful I had a mom who raised me with chores and responsibilities in the home. I've always been able to do domestic jobs because of my early training. When Emilie and I got married, I loved helping her with food preparation, setting the table properly, clearing off the dirty dishes, loading the dishwasher, running a load of laundry, ironing if needed, and so forth. Boy, I am glad I knew how to do all of these things when Emilie came down with cancer and had to have a bone marrow transplant 13 years ago. She wasn't able to do most of her "domestic engineering" responsibilities for four and a half years. If I hadn't learned all of the inside-the-home responsibilities, our household would have been crippled. But because I'd learned along the way how to function in the home, I was able to carry on our daily activities without having to hire someone to come in to assist me in caring for Emilie and our home.

A cute story came about through this experience. One of Emilie's lady friends from out of town would periodically come to spend a weekend with us to give me a break. She observed that I knew how to do everything regarding keeping a home functioning. It made her wonder what her husband would do if she got sick for any length of time. She went home and shared how I was able to do everything in the home, from menu planning to ironing the clothes. She asked her husband what he would do if she got sick. He thought for a moment and answered, "I'd go live with Bob!"

Friend, I encourage you to invest in your relationships daily. If you're not married, there are plenty of other relationships in your life in which to practice service and kindness. Don't sit back in that recliner and let life pass you by as loved ones and friends are neglected. Youthful living can't be a part of your reality if you decide that growing old means growing distant from the people God has placed in your life.

Engage in your growth as a godly man, and you will be more engaged in your role as a child of God, a man, a husband, a father, and a grandfather.

YOUR GUIDE TO LIVING YOUNG

Do you know what one of the best aspects of a youthful perspective is? You know you're not done. Some people hit a certain age, blow a certain number of candles out, and think they've either arrived or they're all they will ever be. They think they're finished with accomplishing or doing, and there is nothing left to pursue. Both views are settling for less than God's best. When we have a youthful perspective about marriage and life, we get the benefit of wisdom from experience and the blessing of believing that purpose and passion are intended to be a part of our experience now. What view do you take?

1. Do you recognize you are a work in progress? What areas do you sense you need to work on when it comes to marriage and relationships?

2. Did you have examples of lasting, loving relationships when you were growing up? What did you learn from the presence of or absence of strong relationships?

3. If you're married, what rituals of kindness and connection can you restore in your relationship with your wife?

4. After talking to your wife, what are three or four of her specific needs you can work on meeting?

5. If you aren't married or you're widowed, what are ways you can serve your current relationships?

6. Do you have a living-young perspective in your friendships or do you have a grumpy-old-man "can't be bothered" attitude?

7. If you've disengaged in any way from your marriage or your path of purpose, how can you get back to experiencing a full life?

PaPa Bob's Prayer

God, make me a man, husband, father, friend, and mentor of honor. Help me see the ways I can submit to You by submitting my heart to service and care for others. I want to be a strong man of compassion who is quick to pray and quick to follow Your guidance in how I can serve others.

Encourage me to seek ways to serve my wife by being a godly man. Show me what is missing in my marriage and give me the humility to be the one to reach out, step up, and dive into being part of the solution. When I get distracted by my troubles or fears, restore to me a sense of servanthood. Guide me back to what matters—showing Your love to the people I love. Thank You, God, for each and every relationship in my life. Amen.

❧ A Legacy Moment ❧

by *Bradley Joe Barnes* (Bob's grandson)

PaPa's Adventure Field Trips

- PaPa Bob has given all his grandchildren a legacy of fun and togetherness. As a young boy I loved it when PaPa announced we were going on one of his famous "Adventure Field Trips." He took us to the best places for the best experiences. We went to an aquarium, to football games, to Lakers basketball games, and many more special outings.

- One of my favorite trips was when I was seven years old. We all went to Palm Springs. Grammy took all the girls to the spa for pampering, so PaPa announced the boys were going on an adventure. We piled into the van and drove off into the desert. After 30 minutes or so, he exited onto an old dirt road. Dust was flying behind us, and we teased him about being lost. "Just sit back and relax," he ordered with a grin. In just a few more minutes, we came upon a palm-tree-lined oasis. An art fair was being held with plenty of exhibits and artisans doing their artwork. They invited us to join in and create with them. We made beautiful clay pots for Grammy and Mom, but most of all we made great memories.

- Now, 14 years later, I'm still inspired and encouraged by recollections of how my cousins and I enjoyed the treasures of time and adventures with PaPa!

When It Comes to Family, Everything Is Relative!

For this reason I bow my knees before the Father, from whom every family in heaven and on earth derives its name, that He would grant you, according to the riches of His glory, to be strengthened with power through His Spirit in the inner man, so that Christ may dwell in your hearts through faith; and that you, being rooted and grounded in love, may be able to comprehend with all the saints what is the breadth and length and height and depth, and to know the love of Christ which surpasses knowledge, that you may be filled up to all the fullness of God.

Ephesians 3:14-19

You're a man of a certain age. I know this because you have this book in your hand. And you are a man who likes the idea of living young and living a full life all the days of your existence on earth. We have that in common. But it isn't always easy to embrace getting older, is it? There are challenges, obstacles, and times when we feel like the world is made only for the young. But that's not true. God is in the business of creating people of purpose. Every one of us has that in common. What we do about our God-given purpose is up to us. Will we walk with God? Will we build a house on the foundation of God's wisdom? Will we share a legacy of eternal treasure with our families and friends? We have a lot of opportunities to say yes to God's calling on our lives.

What's it going to be? Should we keep going with the great work and privilege of loving others and sharing the knowledge of God's truths? It starts at home, you know. Like everything else that matters, if God's truths are presented, encouraged, modeled, and valued in the home, they become part of each family member's inheritance.

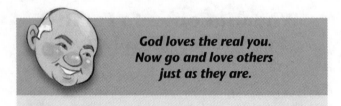

**God loves the real you.
Now go and love others
just as they are.**

What a relief to know God accepts us where we are and as we are. We please Him when we receive what His Son, Jesus Christ, did for us on the cross. It's a personal relationship, pure and simple. Relate to your family with this same love and grace!

What we are in our hearts and who we are in our homes relate significantly to the well-being of our families. All we do, say, and become tie into and reflect how we are choosing to live out our legacy of a lasting, meaningful faith. The way we respond to a grandchild's joke or story about a caterpillar reflects our patience and desire to know that child. The way we support and encourage our wives and their gifts reflects how much we value love and partnership. The way we open our tables to visiting friends, neighbors, those in need, and strangers shows how we respond to Christ's love.

What Is a Home?

Legacy builders make provisions that transform their built-by-people houses into homes filled with love. Yep, home is more than just a place to eat and sleep. What's the difference between a "house" and a "home"? We hear people interchange these two words all the time. But those of us who are fortunate to live in homes know the difference. A home is not simply four walls with a roof overhead. It's not just a structure in an upscale neighborhood. In fact, many homes are found in poor neighborhoods. It doesn't have to have a certain architectural style or construction. Many homes are plain.

Home is built with more than bricks, mortar, lumber, and nails because it is a state of mind. A home is always built with a lot of love. The collective size of the hearts of the people inside this place is more important than the size of the building. Home is a place where we know we are loved and protected. It is a trauma center where hurt people can get well. It is a place where freedom rings. The occupants aren't shaped with the same cookie cutter. Each person is encouraged to grow in his or her direction or bent. In this place called home, we can cry when we are sad and laugh with shouts of joy when we experience victories.

This wonderful haven called home is where we gather to celebrate life. Traditions are carried on, parties are held for special events, and food is shared in fellowship. A home is a place grown children are always glad to come back to.

Home Has an Open Door

When our homes are open as our children grow up and, eventually, expand the family tree, we have chances to share even more of our journeys with them and have opportunities to experience their journeys as they share with us. We are never too old to have a positive effect on those who come after us.

As parents and grandparents, we have direct influence on our children and grandchildren. If we don't have children, we still have direct influence on the people and their children in our lives. I'm sure there are young parents with young kids at our churches and in our neighborhoods that could use help and positive interactions. There will always be people around us who we can treat like beloved family members as we walk out our Christian faith and provide examples of integrity and meaning. We have a lasting legacy we can pass on that extends beyond our immediate families.

Opportunities to continue our legacy exist even when our children move away and we spend more time with our peers. There are still many sets of eyes watching how we live. We can live and leave a legacy no matter how large or small our circle of interactions becomes.

One way to make all you do relative to your faith and your mission to be "an old guy who lives young and shares his legacy" is to keep the doors of your home open so that the people who come to your porch, your stoop, or your apartment step are welcomed wholeheartedly.

One evening our recently married grandson, Chad, and his bride, Erica, called and wanted to know if they could drop by for a visit and to watch a DVD with us. Of course we said yes. When they came in they said, "It's so good to be here. It smells and feels like home!" Emilie and I looked at each other and smiled. That's what we hoped they would experience—that there's no place like home.

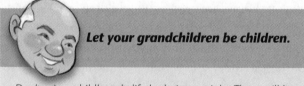

Let your grandchildren be children.

Don't ruin a child's early life by being uptight. There will be times when they spill milk, tear a hole in a shirt, get a lower grade than you would like, use improper English, and so forth. But that's all part of being a child who is learning and growing. Let an ice cream cone drip onto their shirts…or your shirt, for that matter.

On another afternoon, my 25-year-old granddaughter, Christine, and her fiancé, Patrick, asked if they could come over and visit with me. They wanted some advice regarding their upcoming marriage. My immediate response was, "Yes, of course!" After they arrived and we began talking in generalities, Christine had a very serious look upon her face. She asked me one of the most powerful questions about her marriage: "PaPa Bob, would you officiate at Patrick and my wedding?" Wow! What an honor to be asked. I was somewhat taken aback though. My first response after my amazement was, "I can't marry you because I'm not a pastor and I haven't been ordained by the State of California to perform weddings. Thank you, but I can't do it."

At that time Patrick interjected. "No, PaPa! We want only you to marry us!"

How could I refuse such a vote of confidence? I told them that there must be some provision where a citizen could perform such a ceremony—and if so, I would be honored to officiate at their wedding ceremony.

My wife looked me in the eyes and said, "What a compliment for Christine to ask you to marry them. She and Patrick must really respect the man you are!"

Later I called the Orange County Clerk Recorder's office, and they informed me that they did have a provision for such a request. It's called a "Deputy Marriage Commissioner for a Day." I would have to fill out some papers requesting to be deputized for the day of the wedding. So on Sunday afternoon, November 30, 2008, I had the honor of conducting my first wedding ceremony! And it was for my favorite granddaughter (okay, she's my only granddaughter) and her Patrick.

When I was a young man, I would never have thought that my God was big enough to prepare me for such an occasion 50 years down the line. Because of His love and, subsequently, the love of family, these wonderful experiences happen in the sanctuary of my home.

▰▰▰▰ God's "Living Young" Wisdom ▰▰▰▰

We use an old saying in our family: "Use it or lose it!" That's not only a general principle, but it's also a truism of life. When we exercise the gifts that God gives us, we enrich those around us and our resources are multiplied. God has given each of us specific talents and gifts—to some more than others, but to each of us something. We are good stewards when we use these to honor God. Some of us know from personal experience how a stuttering child can become an eloquent speaker or how a brilliant debater can become homeless when he uses his talent slothfully.

Jesus told His disciples that the kingdom of heaven is like a man who called his servants to him before going on a trip. He gave each servant gold coins (Matthew 25:14-30). To one servant he gave five, to another two, and to the third man he gave one coin. Each servant was given according to his ability. The first man traded with his five coins and made five more. The man with two coins did likewise and made two more. But the man with one coin dug a hole in the ground and buried it.

After a long time, the owner of the land came to settle his accounts with the three servants. The first servant brought with him the five coins plus the five he'd earned. The master said, "Well done, good and faithful slave. You were faithful with a few things, I will put you in charge of many things; enter into the joy of your master" (verse 21).

The second man, who had been given two coins, brought forth the two coins plus the two he had made by trading. The master likewise said to him, "Well done, good and faithful slave. You were faithful with a few things, I will put you in charge of many things; enter into the joy of your master" (verse 23).

The third servant came forward with his one gold coin. "Master, I knew you to be a hard man, reaping where you did not sow and gathering where you scattered no seed. And I was afraid, and went away and hid your talent in the ground. See, you have what is yours" (verses 24-25).

The master told him, "You wicked, lazy slave, you knew that I reap where I did not sow and gather where I scattered no seed. Then you ought to have put my money in the bank, and on my arrival I would have received my money back with interest. Therefore take away the talent from him, and give it to the one who has ten talents" (verses 26-28).

The third man didn't mean any harm to the master, but he didn't understand the principles of stewardship and faithfulness. When we are faithful, we are reliable. We show up on time, do what we say we'll do, finish the job we started, and are on the job when we need to be. Jesus ended His parable with, "To everyone who has, more shall be given, and he will have an abundance; but from the one who does not have, even what he does have shall be taken away" (verse 29).

Do you see how this goes right back to the brief-but-effective "use it or lose it" philosophy? We need to use what we've been given for good…for God's glory and purposes.

Friend, this isn't the time to bury what God has given you. Don't hold tightly to what you have to offer because you're afraid or you feel the weight of a limited amount of time. Your family, your friends, your neighbors, your community, and the world at large need men who will invest what they are given by God so that their gifts, finances, unique talents, and godly wisdom serve their marriages, families, homes, friends, churches, and communities. We need men who will take what they've been given and double it so when they stand before Jesus, He will say, "Well done, good and faithful servant! Enter into the joy of My Father!" What a glorious day that will be.

Grandpa's Voice Still Echoes in My Ear

As a boy of nine, I experienced one of my favorite bonding moments with my grandfather J.W. Barnes (on my father's side of the family). He was a robust cotton farmer with hands of steel, a body tough enough for battle, and a heart for God. Every Sunday morning when I was visiting my PaPa, he would take all of us to Anderson Chapel Methodist Church on the outskirts of Anson, Texas.

One Sunday as we began to sing, Papa's voice uttered these words from the hymn "In the Garden" written by Charles Austin Miles in 1912:

> I come to the garden alone
> While the dew is still on the roses
> And the voice I hear falling on my ear
> The Son of God discloses.
>
> *Refrain*
> And He walks with me,
> And He talks with me,
> And He tells me I am His own;
> And the joy we share as we tarry there,
> None other has ever known.

This moment made such an impression on my young boy's heart that the moment has stayed with me for more than seven decades. Hearing my grandfather's strong voice and feeling the might of his faith as he sang to God was very powerful. This great gospel song was written by Charles Miles after reading the Scripture where Mary Magdalene came to the garden and told the disciples she had seen Jesus, her Lord (John 20). Mr. Miles believed in meditating on Scripture. He didn't simply read a passage; no, he would close his eyes and visualize the scene—sometimes even including himself. This is what he did before writing this great hymn of the church. He could see Mary in the garden with Jesus. This vision became the words and music to this wonderful song he wrote.

Quite often as I work in my own garden in the cool of a summer morning before the noonday heat arrives, I catch myself singing the words to this beautiful hymn of faith. The words and melody are soothing to my spirit. I know without a shadow of doubt that God walks with me, and He talks with me, and He tells me I am His own.

You know, I'm not even sure that my PaPa ever knew of this great legacy he gave me. So often what we do with our grandchildren will be remembered long after we're no longer here. And life comes full circle. My grandson Bradley Joe has a wonderful singing voice. Over the years when he's attended church with me, he usually sits to my right. He also sings with gusto like my PaPa did. A few weeks ago, we were talking about marriage and, out of the clear-blue sky, he asked, "PaPa, would you sing at my wedding?" This caught me by surprise because I don't consider myself a very good singer. I guess that because he stood beside me in church and heard me singing so many times, he figured I was good enough.

His question and the subsequent conversation immediately brought to mind the mentoring example I experienced with my PaPa. God has a way of doing an amazing turnaround in a person's life. Sometimes He even uses parts of us—like an old guy's singing voice—to connect us to family members who have gone on before and to the generations that are following after us. How amazing is our great God!

Break Bread and Break Ground

One of the great traditions of yesteryear that returned great dividends to families was to eat dinner or supper together. A common feature in many strong families today is that they share their evening meal together. Adults, young adults, and even teenagers who possess a healthy sense of being heard and known by their families also attribute time at the family table as a reason for feeling connected to their parents and siblings. Emilie and I have not only heard this expressed by countless people over the years, but we've strived to make sharing meals a priority in our family.

I long for the good old days, when it was common practice for families to sit down together in the evening. Many times those families also started their days together at the breakfast table. Some of our family's greatest legacy moments came when we gathered together to break bread. Often this was the time when the children let down their reticence and shared really big things going on in their lives. I find it sad that family meals are becoming a tradition of the past for so many people today. But rather than lament the loss, I'd rather do my part in continuing to make such gatherings a priority for my family, my extended family, and for the people Emilie and I interact with.

In this season of our lives, we might not have family around as regularly, but when we have an opportunity to come together as a family, a simple way to connect with each other is to share a meal. The chances are that our grown children and grandchildren live farther away than we wish they did. They are no doubt busy and consumed with the needs and activities their own growing families are facing. It might seem out of reach to return to the table as an extended family, but I encourage you to consider doing this. If you are on your own and preparing the house and meal seem daunting, why not invite your family to join you at a special restaurant? Or have each person bring a dish and let a family potluck become a new tradition.

Whether for a holiday, a family occasion, or "just because," invite your family to come together. And if your family doesn't include kids and grandkids, consider gathering an enjoyable group of friends to break bread together. This can be just as wonderful. I've heard it said that our friends are the family we choose, so don't forget to nurture those relationships.

However you decide to bring gathering at a table back in fashion, know that your desire to break bread with community and family will break ground on a new set of traditions. Think of Jesus and how He chose to share a special meal with His 12 disciples during His final days. That fellowship with these dearest of earthly companions must have given Him great comfort as He prepared for the trials ahead. Your table at home or a special spot at a restaurant you enjoy will be the gathering place for your most beloved earthly companions. Everyone will receive nourishment, both physical and spiritual!

When it comes to family, everything is relative. When we break bread together, share about what is going on in our lives, and honor one another by listening closely, we nurture more than the body. We also feed the soul and prepare ourselves and others for living full, productive lives.

Your Guide to Living Young

An open door with a welcome mat in front of it is a great sight to see. If you and your family have been more reserved about sharing your space in the past, consider finding ways during this season of life to invite people into your life and home. Even if you don't have close family nearby, if you pray for opportunities to be that welcoming space for others, it will happen.

I know a lot of older gentlemen living on their own who don't feel like they are quite able to make their house space feel like home. I will tell you right now that a woman's touch is always great, but we men are able to create a welcoming area too. Don't sell yourself short.

Be someone who cares about family—including other people's families. Look around your neighborhood, your apartment building, your church and consider who might need encouragement or a listening ear. Asking someone about his family is not only an invitation to talk about what matters in life, but it is a chance to show that person you care. He will get excited about sharing and will be reminded of how important family is. If you've ever asked other grandparents if they have pictures of their grandkids, you know just what I mean.

1. Staying strong in your faith is relevant to all aspects of your family life. In what ways do you lead by example?

2. Who can you take time to ask about his or her family this week? Perhaps that person has an important prayer request about a loved one that you can follow up on.

3. Have you considered hosting a men's group in your home? A generation of young fathers or middle-aged men need our generation to keep communicating with them about family, priorities, and commitments.

Don't forget to be vulnerable with your family. Show them it is okay to open up about struggles and dreams. Become a safe shelter for your family to go to when they have questions or need prayer and guidance.

PaPa Bob's Prayer

Lord, I have let other concerns take priority over my family in the past. Don't let me do the same during these important years. Renew my confidence in You so I am bold in presenting my faith and courageous enough to stand tall for what matters most to me.

My family and those people who have become my family deserve to be shown respect and love. Help me be a great listener and observer so I can encourage them to seek Your strength. Lead me, God. Show me how to keep an open door and an open heart even when I'm afraid or uncertain. I want to be a man whose actions show Your love and the gospel message. Amen.

6

Sometimes We Have to Lose Our Grip to Gain Our Balance

Give us this day our daily bread.

Matthew 6:11

One of the secrets to having a fulfilling life fueled by youthful energy is to have wholesome balance. It takes many people a long time to discover the importance of good balance and healthy boundaries. Some guys never figure it out. I've encountered peers who do too much or try to be too many things for people. I've found myself in conversations with others who were trying to remedy their past lack of balance by restricting their willingness to commit to anyone or anything now. It seems that even the pursuit of balance requires balance!

Being or doing too much becomes a negative. It's finding the balance in the middle that evens out the extreme highs and the extreme lows. God might ask us to let go of more than a few goals, dreams, and weaknesses so we can have a steadier walk of faith. As we study the life of Jesus, we notice that He was involved in a lot of activities. He's not always teaching, praying, or healing. According to the sixth chapter of Mark, we find Jesus...

- "going around the villages teaching" (verse 6). Doing various tasks was routine in His life. Notice in most situations Jesus was serving people.

- "summoned the twelve and began to send them out in pairs" (verse 7). Jesus was involved with people. He was very relational with those He met.

- "in a boat…[in] a secluded place" with His disciples (verse 32). Jesus said to them, "Come away by yourselves to a secluded place and rest a while" (verse 31). Privacy and rest was a big part of His life. He knew that big crowds sapped His energy, and He wanted to be ready for the tasks at hand. He valued His privacy and rest. He also cared for His followers. He wanted His disciples ready for the grueling hours and energy drain they too would experience.

These three areas of our busy lives also need to be addressed if we are going to develop balance:

- tasks
- relationships
- privacy, including rest

If these areas were of concern for Jesus, they are of concern in our lives. We need to tend to them through prayer and with godly wisdom. When our lives are centered on God, we are much more energized and content!

Trust More Than We Fear

Trusting God completely is significant. Does the thought of trusting so much initially scare you or does it give you comfort? It isn't easy to trust unconditionally, but the way to find our balance during this time of life requires that we let go of our grip on fear (or fear's grip on us!) and hold tightly to God's promises.

Emilie and I have witnessed time and again how fear invades people's thoughts and actions as they get older. Soon that fear impacts their motives and decisions because the fear and subsequent distrust become their guides instead of faith and trust. Psalm 127:1-2 says,

> Unless the LORD builds the house,
> They labor in vain who build it;
> Unless the LORD guards the city,
> The watchman keeps awake in vain.
> It is vain for you to rise up early,
> To retire late,
> to eat the bread of painful labors;
> For He gives to His beloved even in his sleep.

Half of knowing what you want is knowing what you're willing to give up to get it.

Sit down and think about what the cost might be to achieve your main desire. Sometimes you might conclude you aren't willing to pay the price. Remember, every goal has a price. Release anything from your life that compromises your faith, your family, or you.

The English Standard Version Bible translates the second to last line as "eating the bread of anxious toil." We eat this bread when we're busy making our impression on the world and falling short on one of the main investments that really count—our families. If we operate from the belief that our care depends all on our actions rather than on God's provision, we will find ourselves eating "the bread of anxious toil." And it will not ever be satisfying.

This lesson is even harder to embrace during this time of life when we're working less or not at all. All the routines, efforts, and hard labor we depended on to keep ourselves afloat are no longer an active part of our lives. So what are we to do? Well, we can worry or we can wait on the Lord, trusting Him. We need not live on "anxious toil." Scripture tells us that God will take care of us. If our priorities are correct, we can give quality time to our families, communities, and churches without worrying about what will happen tomorrow. And we set our best priorities by following God's Word. Matthew 6:33 says, "Seek first [God's] kingdom and His righteousness, and all these things [everything you need] will be added to you." And I can attest that God is certainly capable of keeping His promises!

Trusting God for Daily Bread

Our simplest needs are our greatest needs—food, shelter, relationships. These God will provide for us. Food on our table—bread—is about as basic as it can get. Jesus gives several examples of what we should include in our prayers:

> When you pray, go into your inner room, close your door and pray to your Father who is in secret, and your Father who sees what is done in secret will reward you. And when you are praying, do not use meaningless repetition as the Gentiles do, for they suppose that they will be heard for their many words. So do not be like them; for your Father knows what you need before you ask Him. Pray, then, in this way: "Our Father who is in heaven, hallowed be Your name. Your kingdom come. Your will be done, on earth as it is in heaven. Give us this day our daily bread. And forgive us our debts, as we also have forgiven our debtors. And do not lead us into temptation, but deliver us from evil. [For Yours is the kingdom and the power and the glory forever. Amen.]" (Matthew 6:6-13, brackets in original).

Jesus knew how important food was for His followers (including us!). He also knew that Moses was told by God that bread would rain down from heaven (manna) for the Israelites. God instructed the Israelites to gather just enough for one day's need, except on the sixth day when they were to gather enough for two days, so they could rest and do no work on the seventh day (Exodus 16:4-5). This was a test from God to see if the Israelites would do as He commanded and if they would choose to trust Him for their daily provision. After a short while, the Israelites complained about the manna God provided. They also broke the rules and tried to collect more than they needed for their daily allotment. In essence, they didn't trust God!

In many ways, we're not much different today. We essentially face the same two tests in our daily walk with God that the Israelites did:

- Will we follow God's principles?
- Will we trust God for our daily provision?

And when things are going right, we generally feel okay about going along with God. But the moment things turn sour or don't go how *we* want them to, we stop trusting God's timetable and want to take back control (as much as possible, anyway). But that's where faith comes in. Faith always travels hand in hand with hope. Faith enables us to keep our hopes up when the road becomes rocky or more obscure. Faith is what we need to keep moving on, keep moving up, and keep trusting our heavenly Father—trusting that what we go through is worthwhile.

God's promises for providing daily bread were true for the Israelites during the Exodus and the subsequent 40 years of wilderness travel (see the book of Exodus), and they certainly hold true for us today. He didn't promise He would give us all of our daily "wants," but He did promise He would provide for our daily "needs." Sometimes it might not seem to be all we need, but it is. I remember a story Emilie's mother shared about her childhood in New York City. Times were so hard, and they didn't always know where their next meal was coming from. Her mother (Emilie's grandmother) on many occasions would make "rock soup" for dinner. It was a very simple recipe:

- 1 pot
- 1 quart of water (bring to a boil)
- 6-7 small rocks
- A dash of salt and pepper
- 1 dash of ketchup
- 4 small soup bowls

That was it. They pretended they were eating real food. Somehow that was enough.

Jesus declared, "I am the bread of life. Whoever comes to me will never go hungry, and whoever believes in me will never be thirsty" (John 6:35 NIV). God will provide. That is our basic test. Do we believe He will do as He says? Will God provide? The Israelites didn't believe, and they wandered in the desert for 40 years before they were allowed to enter the "Promised Land."

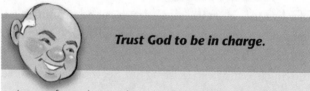

Trust God to be in charge.

Let go of your desire to be right all the time. Sometimes God might be trying to teach you something through someone you might not see eye to eye with. Listen up.

One of the Barnes' family traditions is to bow in prayer before each meal. This is so we will never forget that God is the provider of our daily bread. Whether we're at home or in a fancy restaurant, we all join hands and thank God for His faithfulness. How do you show your faith and trust in God to provide for all your needs? How do you give God thanks? How do you show your family how much you depend on Him for every need you have?

GOD'S "LIVING YOUNG" WISDOM

If you can't trust, you won't receive the blessing of trust. It takes courage to trust others, and we need to use discernment in selecting those who will respect our willingness to trust them. Trust can have a price tag, as all things of worth in life usually do. It's called risk.

Thankfully, there is no risk in trusting God for needs, spiritually, mentally, and physically. We can go to Him with all our weaknesses, failings, sins, and broken hearts and seek His grace. God is trustworthy!

When King David realized his sin in having an affair with Bathsheba, he turned to God, confessed, and prayed for forgiveness. I consider this one of the greatest prayers in all of Scripture. David knew he could trust God—and that God would accept his confession. Look at his cry for help:

> Have mercy on me, O God,
>   according to your unfailing love;
> according to your great compassion
>   blot out my transgressions.
> Wash away all my iniquity and
>   cleanse me from my sin.
> For I know my transgressions,
>   and my sin is always before me.
> Against you, you only, have I sinned
>   and done what is evil in your sight;
> so you are right in your verdict
>   and justified when you judge.
> Surely I was sinful at birth,
>   sinful from the time my mother conceived me.

> Yet you desired faithfulness even in the womb;
>   you taught me wisdom in that secret place…
> Create in me a pure heart, O God,
>   and renew a steadfast spirit within me.
> Do not cast me from your presence
>   or take your Holy Spirit from me.
> Restore to me the joy of your salvation
>   and grant me a willing spirit, to sustain me
>   (Psalm 51:1-6,10-12).

King David presents his heartfelt confession and expresses his sorrow as well as his need for cleansing. He trusts God with his brokenness. David knows he can only be restored to wholeness and balance through God's forgiveness. We can learn a lot from his pursuit of God's help. David goes to God with vulnerability, respect, and awareness of God's great awesomeness. All those emotions we have when we realize we've been following the world instead of our Lord and decide to turn back to God. Ultimately, David stands firm in his belief that God is faithful to hear him and respond to his cry for mercy. We need to do the same.

Trust in Relationships

Our quest for balance as we walk toward godly priorities is aided by the help of others we trust. When we exercise our "trust muscle," we accept these people for who they are. If we nurture our relationships and bring both wisdom and grace to them, our friendships provide opportunities to be honest with other people or a small group of men. It also means they can be honest with us. It goes both ways in solid friendships. When there is mutual trust, we hear our friends when they offer constructive criticism and gentle spiritual advice.

The apostle Paul wrote a strong letter to the church in Corinth, and the church members accepted his words of correction because they knew Paul cared deeply for their souls and their well-being.

He wasn't trying to put them down or build himself up. Instead, Paul trusted that what he shared with them would be accepted as godly correction and instruction sent via his loving heart. Often it takes a true friend to share with us about our "blind side." We all have them, but not everyone will have enough confidence or be in a position where they're allowed to let us know what we aren't noticing about ourselves.

Wisdom from the book of Ecclesiastes is often used in marriage ceremonies because it stresses the importance or value of having another person active in our lives. One favorite passage reads:

> Two are better than one, because they have a good return for their labor: If either of them falls down, one can help the other up. But pity anyone who falls and has no one to help them up. Also, if two lie down together, they will keep warm. But how can one keep warm alone? Though one may be overpowered, two can defend themselves. A cord of three strands is not quickly broken (4:9-12 NIV).

God gives us great encouragement through the friendships He's blessed us with. These relationships help us better understand the importance of trusting God. If we trust our friends, how much more can the God of the universe who loves us be trusted! Our human connections give us great insights into our relationship with Christ.

Lose the Negative Words

For those of us seeking balance and wholeness, the topic of anger has to be addressed. When we release our frustration through unkind words or raised voices, we hurt others and often lose our own objective perspective. Our surges of emotion and harmful words are often used to take control of a situation. Having control over people in this way will, in the end, throw our spiritual and emotional health off balance. It will also wound the people involved.

Words can be good, pure, and wholesome or they can be negative, mean-spirited, and extremely harmful. No matter what we do, where we are, what we're involved in, we all need to make sure we use our words to help people and build them up. We want to select words that ably describe what we mean and what we hope to accomplish. The apostle Paul wrote these warnings to the church in Ephesus: "Let no unwholesome word proceed from your mouth, but only such a word as is good for edification according to the need of the moment, so that it will give grace to those who hear" (Ephesians 4:29).

We need to take time to evaluate our speech periodically. Do we use words that build up people? Are we in the habit of using words that tear down people? Do our words discourage people or encourage them?

Jesus covered another aspect of our speech when He warned believers to not make oaths. He said we should answer any question with a yes or a no without adding an emphasis, such as "by heaven" or "by the earth." Jesus said, "Let your statement be, 'Yes, yes' or 'No, no'" (Matthew 5:37).

Have you ever heard of people getting in trouble for something they didn't say? During military combat, American soldiers are instructed to provide only their name, rank, and serial number if they are taken prisoner and questioned by the enemy. (This is partly because the United States ratified the Geneva Convention III established in 1949.) I've also heard that in medical school students are instructed to weigh carefully their words spoken during operations in case the patient can register what is said. As the anesthetic is given, anxiety may strike a patient if they hear the surgeon say, "I'm not feeling very confident today."

Within our families, the need for using care with our words is the same. Our words need to lift up those we love, not tear them down. It is wise not to say much during times of anger. Words, once said, are impossible to take back, and some words continue to cause pain for many years.

"Be quick to hear, slow to speak and slow to anger" (James 1:19). In today's world of busyness, many of us are more comfortable doing instead of being. Consequently, we prefer to speak instead of listen. A guiding principle in the Barnes family is "You never have to apologize for words you never say." If we all listened more than we spoke, we'd have less opportunities to be tripped up on our own ramblings and more opportunities to truly hear and get to know people.

Keeping Our Words Upbeat

Any words spoken need to be covered in love. Am I saying a couple can never argue? No. We can argue, but we need to set ground rules ahead of time. One good rule is "Don't attack the other person with hurtful dialog." One of the ways Emilie and I have filled our speech with love is in the careful choice of the words we use with each other. We like the two lists Denis Waitley included in his book *The Seeds of Greatness Treasury*. He shares what words we should forget and what words we should remember for loving conversations.

Words to Forget	Words to Remember
I can't	I can
I'll try	I will
I have to	I want to
I should have	I will do
I could have	My goal
Someday	Today
If only	Next time
Yes, but	I understand
Problem	Opportunity
Difficult	Challenging
Stressed	Motivated
Worried	Interested

Impossible	Possible
I, me, my	You, your
Hate	Love[1]

My friend, are there some words in your vocabulary you need to eliminate and replace with words that affirm your love and deepen intimacy? I encourage you to let your "yes be yes" and your "no be no." Like Paul said, "Let all bitterness and wrath and anger and clamor and slander be put away from you, along with all malice" (Ephesians 4:31).

Watch your language. Communicate using positive, loving words. If your words are not edifying, switch gears in your mind and your mouth and speak only words worth remembering. Negative words kill the spirit; positive words build up and encourage.

Your Guide to Living Young

You can trust God with every physical, spiritual, emotional, and relational need. Go to Him when you need forgiveness and when you need guidance. Show your trust in God by praising His name in all circumstances. Lose your grip on pride and release your strong desire to control everything. This is how you will be able to live a balanced, godly life. Spend time with the Lord and get to know Him intimately. Ask for His leading and correction in your life. Pray that He will bring godly men into your life so you can develop strong friendships with people you can trust and who have wisdom to share for your journey.

1. What are you reluctant to let go of so you can trust God more completely?
2. When have you struggled to do things in your own power and realized that God had a better plan of action?

3. Have you ever done a "trust fall exercise"? That's where you let yourself fall backward and trust the other people to catch you? Consider whether you've done this with God.

4. Which friendships or acquaintances would you like to invest time in?

5. Who will tell you the truth when you need to hear it?

PaPa Bob's Prayer

God, give me a clean heart today. Out of fear and pride, I have sought the things of the world more than I have pursued You and Your truths. Help me let go of those areas of life that keep me from fully trusting You and those needs that bind me to worldly priorities. I want to focus on Your priorities so my life will be balanced and whole. Guide me toward wisdom through the good and godly friends You bring into my life and through Your living Word.

I trust You with my needs today, Lord. I also trust You with my future. Forgive me for trying to take control of every detail because I'm afraid of what tomorrow might bring. Thank You for Your peace and for the contentment and satisfaction that follows when I submit to Your will and trust in Your provision. Amen.

❦ A Legacy Moment ❦

by *Chad Merrihew* (Bob's grandson)

- I am so blessed to have PaPa in my life. I am still young and have so much ahead of me, but not a day goes by that I don't quote my grandfather. Our family has been through a lot. When I have times of doubt or fear, I look to my grandparents for reassurance.

- The reason our family is so strong for each other and in the Lord is because of PaPa Bob and Grammy Emilie. When I think of them, I think of Moses and his wife. They lived true, devoted lives that were pleasing to God. And when their lives ended, the Lord told Moses that because of his faith the generations to follow would be blessed.

- I know the Lord blesses my life and my future because of the legacy of faith and family my grandparents have shaped for us every day of their lives.

Bob, Emilie and the grandkids enjoy a day of living young. Pictured from left to right are Weston, Chad, Christine, Emilie, Bevan, Bob, Bradley Joe.

7

Get into Movies Cheap, but Don't Forget to Live Rich

Do not cast me off in the time of old age; do
not forsake me when my strength fails.

Psalm 71:9

At some time in our personal journey, we will be tempted to use the excuse that we're too old to play an important part in anyone's life again. We might resist being active even when our involvement is very important. We see a stranded motorist needing help, we see a child being picked on by a bully, or we see our loved ones struggling to find their way, but we hold back because we either think we can't be helpful or we've decided we're too old to get involved anymore. Either scenario is settling for less than this season of life offers.

Is There Such a Thing as "Too Old"?

When is too old "too old"? When we're young we want everyone to know that we are 10½ or almost 15. I remember on my tenth birthday, my mother told me to act a certain way because I was almost 11. But there comes a time in life when those fractions aren't important. In fact, at 70 we want to enjoy that age for the 365 full days. I've never heard a 70-year-old say he's 70½. In youth the fractions are important; in the older years they aren't.

When I taught world history, my students were introduced to an explorer named Juan Ponce de León. This Spanish explorer set sail to find the Fountain of Youth. There was a rumor in the European world about a water source that kept people young. Here we are, more than 700 years later, and we're still looking for a way to turn back time through water. If you don't believe that, just check out the water section of your local grocery store. Shelf after shelf is lined with water-based liquids that claim to give people more energy, power, or at least a better start to our days or workouts.

The possibility that we can extend our lives has great appeal, but seldom can we do that by following the tangents of suspect promises and claims. And is trying to return to our youth really what will give us satisfaction? I think not. Our age and experience has great value! And if you still question that, then this book is timely for you.

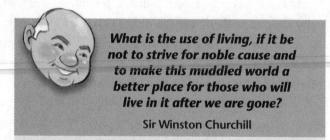

What is the use of living, if it be not to strive for noble cause and to make this muddied world a better place for those who will live in it after we are gone?

Sir Winston Churchill

The Bible says there are two types of people—the takers and the givers. The givers have the riches and the more meaningful life. It is better to give than to receive.

Even at our age we struggle with the "needs vs. wants" in life. However, Scripture teaches us to be content where we are in life. The apostle Paul wrote, "I am not saying this because I am in need, for I have learned to be content whatever the circumstances" (Philippians 4:11 NIV). We are never too old to embrace a bigger faith and experience a richer, more vibrant life. Stay tuned for more good news about how we can live young during our retirement years. We'll also discover many riches of this season of life along the way.

We Are Classics

In our area in Southern California, there are car shows on any given Saturday or Sunday morning. Some of the vehicles are new; some are classics—restored and looking like the day they came off the assembly line. Do you know which ones get the most attention? That's right. The *old* classics. The biggest crowds are bunched around these beauties. Why? Because they remind us of the way life used to be when the country was producing cars with very unique styles and designs. We are a lot like those classic cars! We have our own style and design, and in our own ways we can shine with the best of the new models. We just have to find out how we shine the brightest.

The younger models are the whippersnappers who can learn from us, right? That is, if we are good examples. You might be surprised by what people notice about you and when they notice it. I've had men share they've learned from me how to take care of a sick wife because of watching how I have helped Emilie during her long battle against cancer. So while we're living out our faith as men of God, there are people paying attention.

We old-timers have valuable experiences! Be willing to be positive examples for any of the younger generation who are looking. One day (faster than they think), they will be the senior citizens who take the lead. But right now, young people can learn so much from us—we who have experienced failures and successes in our journeys on this earth. Even in losses there are crucial lessons to be gained. Make each phase of life a teaching moment. How we react to victories and defeats will not go unnoticed. God has a purpose even in the extremes of a life cycle. The riches of these experiences can be mined and shared with people who have not yet encountered the large numbers of victories or moments of defeat we have just by virtue of living a long time.

Emilie and I have several friends who retired, traveled extensively, played golf and tennis, and ate fine food. After a short while, they looked at each other and asked, "Is this all there is?" Retirement gives us great opportunities to do what we've always wanted to do but never had the time to do them. We can start a small business we've always wanted to do, travel out-of-state to where our children and grandchildren live, go on short mission trips, serve food at homeless shelters, or volunteer for nonprofit organizations. The important thing is to not stay home and sit in the corner. Get out and live! Life is full of changes, and so is this period of life.

**It is not length of life,
but depth of life.**

Ralph Waldo Emerson

Don't live the same life for 60 to 80 years. Step out and make each day, month, and year a new adventure. Don't wait for tomorrow; make the most of today.

God's "Living Young" Wisdom

One of the little-known personalities in the Bible is a man by the name of Barzillai. This 80-year-old man is mentioned briefly in 2 Samuel. He helped David and his men when they were fleeing from Absalom and his army. Without Barzillai's role in aiding David, history would have been different. We don't know much about Barzillai, except he lived in a small village and was wealthy. When he and a few villagers brought food and clothing to David and his men, his efforts were greatly appreciated by the king. In fact, after Absalom was killed and David went back to Jerusalem, he specifically sought out Barzillai in his small village east of the Jordan River. He invited this faithful volunteer to come with him to Jerusalem and live as his guest for the rest of his life.

Even though he was appreciative of David's offer, Barzillai said no thanks. His reasoning was that at 80, he was too old to move and leave his friends behind.

> Barzillai said to the king, "How long have I yet to live, that I should go up with the king to Jerusalem? I am now eighty years old. Can I distinguish between good and bad? Or can your servant taste what I eat or what I drink? Or can I hear anymore the voice of singing men and women? Why then should your servant be an added burden to my lord the king?" (2 Samuel 19:34-35).

When this old man took action and did what he could do, God used his efforts. The same can be true for us as in every circumstance and at every age. Who knows what lies ahead? All we need to do is what is placed before us. We must just be available to God for His purpose, whether it be small or huge. Let's not use old age as an excuse that prevents us from doing marvelous things. We can and will serve others, and we will honor God in the process!

Being a Good Steward of Money

An elderly woman said to her husband, "I wish I had enough money, time, and courage to get a face-lift…My face is drooping!" Her beloved husband said, "Dear, the most inexpensive and lasting face-lift is just to smile. It draws your facial features upward, and that is what draws people to you." During this period of our lives, we can choose to be content. As I've noted before, the apostle Paul wrote,

> I have learned to be content in whatever circumstance
> I am. I know how to get along with humble means,
> and I also know how to live in prosperity; in any and
> every circumstance I have learned the secret of being
> filled and going hungry, both of having abundance
> and suffering need. I can do all things through Him
> who strengthens me (Philippians 4:11-13).

Many people, if given a lot of money, would find more ways to lose it than to make it multiply. That's because discontentment creeps into people when they have little and when they have a lot. If people are unhappy with what they have, more money or more possessions won't change that attitude. Paul said he learned to be content in whatever circumstance he was in. He knew what it was like to go hungry, be in pain, and be imprisoned; yet, he still spoke of being content. If we skip a meal, or at least if I do, I get irritated or even angry. How about you?

Contentment plays a part in how well we handle our money. One of the hardest principles to grasp and teach is financial discipline. In modern industrial societies, we are nations of spenders and consumers. Most know little about the importance of saving. But to become financially independent, we must spend less than we make. That is hard to do if we keep wanting more so we spend more.

There are many Christian books that can help us establish the discipline to become financially independent, but the bottom-line principles include:

- Save little by little.
- Say no to consumable goods that aren't necessary.
- Develop a plan for saving.
- Spend less than you make.
- Use credit cards only if the balance is paid at the end of each month.

- Give to the Lord's work on a weekly basis.

- Never gamble or play the lottery.

- Take advantage of senior deals and discounts.

- If it sounds too good to be true, it probably is.

- Never buy anything from a solicitor over the phone.

- Be willing to take risks after prayer and receiving wise counsel.

- Believe in yourself and your product.

- Think success.

- Be thankful to God for the opportunities He gives you.

- Do business with people of integrity.

- Be a person of integrity.

The Wealth of Wisdom

Good stewardship ideally begins in the younger years, not when we are thinking about kicking back in retirement. But even those who have planned carefully for their retirement can face very hard times. The recent financial setbacks, worldwide and especially in the United States, caught many older citizens off guard. We thought we had enough savings, pensions, and investments to give us a very comfortable lifestyle. But when the recession came, a lot of people were hit hard in their wallets. Many people in our area who believed they were ready financially to retire comfortably discovered they would have to work another 10 to 15 years just to recoup their losses.

The Bible is full of verses that deal with finances. We are warned that we can't serve two masters:

> If you have not been faithful in the use of unrighteous wealth, who will entrust the true riches to you? And if you have not been faithful in the use of that which is

> another's, who will give you that which is your own?
> No servant can serve two masters; for either he will hate
> the one and love the other, or else he will be devoted to
> one and despise the other. You cannot serve God and
> wealth (Luke 16:11-13).

We often operate on the false assumption that if we have a lot of money, we've lived a successful life. But we're warned that people who want to get rich fall into temptations, traps, and foolish and harmful desires that can plunge them into ruin and destruction (1 Timothy 6:9). God, through the writers of the New Testament, isn't saying we can't or shouldn't have wealth. What He is saying is that we need to make sure money is not our master, not our focus in life. Rather, we should have money as a servant. It serves us; we are not controlled by it. Our God is the giver of all good things! We know where good comes from, so we should be thanking Him. He's given us all good things, and He wants us to be faithful stewards and trustees of them.

Hopefully we've been good stewards of our finances during our prime earning years. Now what principles about money can we follow as we look forward to the rest of our senior years?

Be realistic in our financial planning. Know what we can expect. There are a lot of financial planners who can help us in this area. Continue to save money in a disciplined way. Just because you have the money doesn't mean you should spend it. "Delayed gratification" is a concept many of the younger generations know nothing about, but you and I understand that philosophy as a wise practice. We can't do everything right now, and even if we could, we shouldn't. Lay a good financial foundation and be willing to make disciplined sacrifices. We need to set goals and ask God to give us guidance and wisdom. Being careful with our money and getting several opinions about who we can trust for investments and other decisions go without saying. There are people who try to take advantage of people in our generation.

Stay away from debt. One reason many seniors can't retire as they would like is because they never learned to stay out of debt. I'm not saying we need to cut up our credit cards though. Credit cards are required for many activities these days, including car rentals and hotel reservations. Credit cards can be positive as long as we make sure we pay off the balance at the end of each month. Unfortunately too many seniors have had to declare bankruptcy because they fell into a debt trap by becoming overextended. In our younger days we had the years available to speculate on some investments. We knew if the investments went sour, we could make it up by being more conservative for a few years. However, now that time isn't as readily available, we need to go more conservative by reducing the risks.

Have all paperwork in order. We want to make sure we have all our legal paperwork in order. We don't want our heirs to suffer because of our lack of planning for our inevitable demise. (Yes, all living creatures die at some point.) We want to determine ahead of time what will be done with our possessions. We don't want to leave it up to the state to make those decisions and take a big chunk of any assets. When you have your will, advance directives, trusts, and other financial instruments set up, make sure members of the family know where you keep those documents, who the primary contact person will be, and the phone numbers and addresses of the people who will need to be notified in case of accidents, illness, or end-of-life issues. We should have as many of our possessions as possible put into a trust. Estate plans need to be carefully prayed about, worked through, and drawn up by a professional to make sure everything is covered.

Don't wait another minute. If we haven't planned well up until now, we need to start saving and planning right away. The first order of business is to get rid of debt and seek wise counsel so we can make up for some of the time we've wasted. If we've lost a large chunk of our retirement income and provision because of a financial crisis, we need to take a hard look at where we are and take the steps necessary to get back into the best financial shape possible. Don't be too scared to take the steps needed to start again.

YOUR GUIDE TO LIVING YOUNG

A rich man is someone who recognizes who he is as a man of God. If we know this, we are blessed beyond measure! Even if we don't have a lot of cash to spend, we still have much to share with the people around us.

Think about it. We can spend our time and attention on loved ones, helping people, charitable works, and setting aside quiet moments to commune with God. We can spend satisfying afternoons in gardens or parks appreciating God's great variety of creativity. We can spend time on the phone or at playgrounds with our grandkids. Being this kind of steward with our blessings means we will feel wealthy and satisfied.

God fills and satisfies the soul. We need to not worry about what we don't have. Instead, let's invest in gratitude. That well won't run dry because there is so much to be thankful for, including senior discounts at your local cinema.

1. When have you used your age as an excuse to get out of living richly and boldly? Was it a good idea? What did you miss out on?

2. How can you be a better steward of all God has entrusted to you?

3. Barzillai's small gesture of help turned out to be important to King David. Is there an act of service or kindness, large or small, you've been putting off that could make a difference in someone's life? When will you take charge and get it done?

4. What do you plan to do to make your life more vibrant now that you refuse to use your age as an excuse?

PaPa Bob's Prayer

Father God, thank You for all You've given to me and my family over the years. Protect me from discontentment. Turn my heart toward gratitude when I start to feel sorry for myself or discouraged because of the effects of getting older. Lead me to wise counsel for financial matters. Help me be a good mentor to others who might need advice about being a good steward financially.

Help me to never sell myself short because when I do that, I'm not placing my faith in You and Your plan and purpose for this time of my life. I love You, Lord, and I want to continue to serve You until my last breath is drawn. Amen.

Even Old Bones Can Take a Leap of Faith

A joyful heart is good medicine, but a broken spirit dries up the bones.

Proverbs 17:22

I often hear people say "Have enough faith!" or "I have faith that this will happen!" What do we really mean by the word "faith"? In Hebrews 11:1, we read that faith is the assurance (meaning you have no doubt at all) of things hoped for (much more than hoped for) and the conviction of things not seen. Pastor Andy Stanley says, "Faith is the confidence that God is who He says He is and will do everything He has promised to do." The Christian has two choices on how he views faith:

- as circumstantial faith
- or as Christian faith

Circumstantial faith. This is faith based on how well things go in life. When things go smoothly and it seems our prayers are answered, those holding circumstantial faith claim to believe in and follow God. But when life isn't going so well and troubles arise, these people don't feel as sure about God's continual presence. They try to solve the problems on their own using their own power and cleverness. This fair-weather faith falls apart quickly.

The people with this kind of faith view God as a genie to ask favors of rather than the Lord of all who should be worshipped and obeyed.

Christian faith. Christians who know "God is good all the time" keep their eyes on Jesus, who initiates and perfects our faith. This is the faith I've walked with throughout my life. My knowledge and trust of God doesn't depend on my circumstances. No matter the ups and the downs of life, my faith is in God, who is able to do all He says in Scripture. If He says it in Scripture, that settles it for me. "Fixing our eyes on Jesus, the author and perfecter of faith, who for the joy set before Him endured the cross, despising the shame, and has set down at the right hand of the throne of God" (Hebrews 12:2).

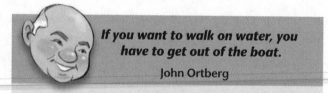

If you want to walk on water, you have to get out of the boat.

John Ortberg

It's easy to be a dreamer, but to take a leap of faith requires leaving the security of routine. Don't be afraid to try something new. Be willing to step out of the boat.

The Lord God is the "Alpha and the Omega, the beginning and the end" (Revelation 21:6). He is the potter, and we are the clay. He knew us before we were born. Yes, even in times of illness, divorce, changes in the economy, death, and failures, we can trust and depend on God. He will never depart from us or forsake us!

In Job 2:9-10, we read the conversation between Job and his wife. She asks him a question regarding the tragic events in their family's life: "Do you still hold fast your integrity? Curse God and die!" But Job replies as a man of true faith: "Shall we indeed accept good from God and not accept adversity?" By Job's reply, we know that he had true faith in God because it went beyond the circumstances of his life.

Which faith do you live by? A faith that depends on circumstances or a faith that stays solid in spite of circumstances?[1]

Where Does Hope Come From?

Is there a time when it's okay to give up hope? One of the most important ways Emilie and I have found to keep our hope alive is to let God be God. Sometimes we miss out on the hope He has for us because we insist on finding it where *we* want to and in the form *we* desire instead of opening our minds and our hearts to receive it as God wants to give it.

We may consciously set our hearts and hopes on happy, fruitful marriages, or a child or two, or a successful career, or being able to live in a certain geographical area. Maybe some of us assume our lives will include certain amenities, such as good health, a happy family, and a comfortable income. If these wishes and desires aren't fulfilled, we may find ourselves feeling disappointed, discouraged, and even abandoned by God instead of feeling joyful and hopeful as we rejoice in His presence. We let our hopes rise according to what we wanted, and we feel let down when life doesn't turn out the way we want. Instead of looking to God, we find ourselves plodding along, going through the motions of living.

How easy it is to miss out on hope when we forget Who is really in charge of the universe and all we hope for! Even with the many disappointments we all face in our life journeys, there are good reasons to keep hope alive. I've learned that if I choose to wait and keep my heart and mind open, hope will come to me in surprising ways. Not necessarily in the form of feeling good or receiving good news, but in a variety of wonderful ways. Perhaps a friend will call to invite me to a baseball game, or a few guys will want me to go deep-sea fishing with them in Mexico, or my church buddies and I will attend a men's retreat in the mountains. These small joys provide the support and encouragement I need as I wait patiently for the fulfillment of my larger hopes. And when God fills them, they may not be exactly what I figured I wanted, but they will connect me more closely to God than getting my own way would.

So how do I keep upbeat when I'm going through difficult times? I keep reminding myself that God is God and I'm not. I let Him do what He does best. He's not a servant at my beck and call. He is God, the Creator of the universe. He's my loving heavenly Father who watches over me and enjoys surprising me.

Hope Despite the Hard Stuff

God promised us a future and a hope (Jeremiah 29:11). Because we trust Him and His Word, we know the treasures He has in store for us will be wonderful. And that knowledge provides comfort and stability during difficult times. Today and tomorrow God's will and plans will unfold. Sometimes that means we have to let go of our "right" to have things just the way we want them or just the way we hope for. We need to trust Him for our hope the same way we trust Him for our daily bread. If we're willing to accept God's terms and wait on Him, the hope He provides is always enough.

In *Tracks of a Fellow Struggler*, Reverend John Claypool describes how lack of hope is not based on truth:

> Despair is always presumptuous. How do we know what lies in the Great Not Yet or how some present "evil" may work itself out as a blessing in disguise?...[I need to] be patient before I label any experience or close the door of hope. Despair is presumption, pure and simple, a going beyond what the facts at hand should warrant...The worst thing is never the last thing. God is already working on Plan B even as Plan A lies in shambles around our feet.[2]

God is beyond the hardest moments of our lives. His peace is bigger and mightier than any trouble we will ever face. We need to reject participating in the guessing game of what "might happen" because it can immerse us in despair. Instead, we want to set our hearts on God's truth, knowing He will be with us always. He is our hope now and forever!

GOD'S "LIVING YOUNG" WISDOM

If we find ourselves out on a limb and we want to reach out and know Jesus, we can draw hope from Zaccheus. He was a wealthy tax collector and very short so he climbed a sycamore tree to see over the crowds when Jesus was passing by. When Jesus saw Zaccheus, He told him to come down because He was going to go to his house (Luke 19:1-10). Another thing we can do is remind ourselves that God loves us. We can take heart from the way God reached out and revealed His all-inclusive love through His interaction with this reviled tax man.

Although Zaccheus will always be remembered for his small physical stature and having to climb a tree to see Jesus, we often overlook the courage he displayed. Wealthy and influential in his society and the city, his profession as a tax collector alienated him from his fellow Jews. So despised were tax collectors, that Luke wrote, "Now all the tax collectors and the sinners were coming near [Jesus] to listen to Him" (Luke 15:1). Wealthy and ruthless, Zaccheus was a rich man monetarily but a poor man among his peers. He was a "successful failure." Though prosperous and powerful, he obviously knew something was missing from his life because he wanted to see Jesus so desperately that he was willing to be undignified and climb a tree.

What caused Zaccheus to climb up a tree and go out on a limb? I believe he knew he didn't know the true meaning of life. He realized he was missing something. He couldn't let this once-in-a-lifetime opportunity pass him by. Being short in stature but great in zeal, he had to climb a tree to see this man called Jesus.

What obstacle did Zaccheus have to overcome? Although he was short, the main obstacle for Zaccheus was the crowd that surrounded Jesus on all sides. We tend to see Zaccheus as the only seeker in this story, but what about Jesus? He didn't just happen to be passing through this small town of Jericho. Jesus said His mission was to seek and save the lost (Luke 15:3-10). I have no doubt that one of the reasons Jesus was in Jericho that day was to seek out a lonely, despised tax collector. And just as He did for Zaccheus, Jesus will meet us where we are so He can offer us forgiveness, salvation, and love.

Let me encourage you to contemplate these points and consider implementing them in your life:

- Realize you have a need.

- Recognize that the answer to your need is Jesus.

- Seek out a believer's friendship so you can learn more about Jesus and living for Him. Everyone can use a mentor in life.

- Get plugged in to a good, Bible-teaching church.

- Develop the habit of reading God's Word every day. I suggest you start with the book of John.

- Really get to know who Jesus is.

- Accept Jesus' offer of salvation and make Him your Lord and Savior. Invite Him into your life.

- Evaluate who and what interferes with your desire to know Jesus more and serve Him. Ask Jesus to help you grow in Him.

Do you feel like you're out on a limb? Take courage! You can reach Jesus from where you are right now!

Think on These Things

In his letter to the believers in Philippi, Paul offers important advice that will help us focus our thoughts on godliness. I believe we need this guidance more than ever today. We're constantly bombarded with images, sounds, and information brought to us or available to us 24/7 through technology. Paul gave the Philippian believers eight things to think about as they continued their walk as followers of Jesus. I believe we should look at each of these things as stop signs...as items we should stop at and reflect on every day. Paul wrote, "Whatever is true, whatever is honorable, whatever is right, whatever is pure, whatever is lovely, whatever is of good repute, if there is any excellence and if anything worthy of praise, dwell on these things" (Philippians 4:8). Did you get all eight items?

1. whatever is true
2. whatever is honorable
3. whatever is right
4. whatever is pure
5. whatever is lovely
6. whatever is of good repute
7. whatever is excellent
8. whatever is worthy of praise

Wow! This means we need to be serious in evaluating everything we see, hear, read, and think about. When we focus on these things, we may find we have some friends, magazines, books, music, and internet offerings we need to eliminate. And, yes, this is a real test of your commitment to Jesus.

When we take on this lifestyle of believing and following Jesus, we are telling ourselves and the people around us that there will be some changes we'll make as we grow spiritually. We are announcing our desire to live intentionally by focusing on what really matters. Author Hope Lyda describes how life priorities become clearer as we get older and wiser:

> You had wanted to become one of those rare grown-ups who delights in being alive. Now you realize this simple quest is more purposeful than an impressive résumé, more pure than perfection, and more wise than naïve notions of "more is better." This is the night you go to bed knowing that prayers are answered.[3]

As you make changes and focus on more godly pursuits, you'll find yourself increasing the times of stillness in your life. A great gift found in our senior years is having more time to devote to thinking on God and all that He deems good. As we grow in our understanding of Him, His grace shapes our lives into new creations and points us in new directions. We don't need to be afraid of silence and stillness. They are real blessings for us and those around us.

Why not set aside some time right now to focus on Jesus? Here are some things you can do as you center on Him:

- Why not take a walk?
- Why not sing a song of praise?
- Why not start reading the book of John?
- Why not call a friend and talk about life and faith?
- Why not write a loving, encouraging note to your spouse, your child, your parents, or a friend?
- Why not take care of that nagging guilt feeling by confessing what you did wrong and asking for forgiveness?

The more you cultivate quiet times with God, the more He will use that time to shape you, transform you, and lead you.

Praying Young

If you're fortunate enough to hear children pray aloud, you've discovered what genuine, heartfelt prayers sound like. Children's prayers aren't flashy, aren't intended to impress anyone, and aren't edited or directed toward the people who might be listening. Their prayers are real conversations with God, complete with tangents and uncertain pauses. What a great example for us in our faith walk. Living young is even more vibrant when we start praying young—from our hearts straight to our audience of One.

When Emilie and I pray, we take turns praying in single words or short phrases for our children and their families, church members who have specific needs or requests, political leaders, neighbors who need to sell their homes, and people we know who are looking for work. We finish each prayer time with "in Jesus' name, amen." Some of our most precious times together are spent praying. Being in communion with God and each other connects us in such an intimate, meaningful way.

We know prayer works because we've seen God move and work. That's why prayer has been and always will be a strong feature of our family life. We have a close friend who prayed for her son every day. This boy had a tendency to cross over the line of good, positive behavior. He once told his mom very seriously, "Please stop praying for me, Mom. Your prayers are interfering with me having fun." This mischievous teenager has now grown into a very nice man who follows Jesus wholeheartedly. He is married to a believing woman, and they are regulars in their church. As a teenager, this guy knew his mother's faithful prayers were putting a hedge of interference around his not-so-good choices.

Who Holds Tomorrow?

We have a routine habit of saying to people, "I'll see you tomorrow," when in reality we should say, "I'll see you tomorrow if the Lord wills." None of us knows if we will be here tomorrow. As time marches on, we should feel fortunate for each day we have here on earth. We're grateful that God holds our tomorrows in His hands. As the book of James reminds us, "You do not know what your life will be like tomorrow" (4:14).

Each day we read our local papers or watch the news on TV and are reminded that our earthly life can end at any moment. Sometimes we read the local obituary columns to see who has passed on. Most of the people are in the 70- to 95-year range, but quite regularly we hear of a young person who has died. One message comes through loud and clear: "We're here today, but we may be gone tomorrow." Life is "a vapor that appears for a little while and then vanishes away" (James 4:14).

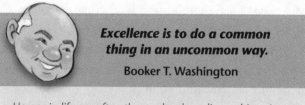

Excellence is to do a common thing in an uncommon way.

Booker T. Washington

Heroes in life are often those who do ordinary things in an unorthodox fashion. They do something differently than most people.

Common sense isn't so common anymore.

Those who prosper do it in an excellent fashion.

Those of us who have accepted Jesus have hope in Him for tomorrow and eternity. On the cross He paid the price for the sins of us all. In believing in Jesus, we have received forgiveness and eternal life by trusting in Him. We can count on Him to follow through on His promises.

Friend, if you've never made the decision to accept Jesus as your personal Savior, I encourage you to do so today. If you need more information, talk to a pastor or a Christian. To accept Jesus and become His follower is easy and straightforward. You just need to confess to Him that you know you aren't perfect—that you are a sinner—and ask for forgiveness. Then ask Him into your life as your Lord, Savior, and source of wisdom and guidance. This should be at the top of your "bucket list"!

▰▰▰ YOUR GUIDE TO LIVING YOUNG ▰▰▰

You're never too old to meet your Lord. You're never too old to take a leap of faith from that limb you're on or from a resting place of inaction. You can have an active, growing, thriving faith. We often hear the word "mature" to nicely describe us at this time in life, don't we? We know people mean "old" though. We might as well face it. But when we consider someone looking at our lives and seeing mature faith in God in action and mature, godly compassion and love being shared with others, that has to be one of the best honors to come our way.

I encourage you to spend time with God in silence. Take time to get to really know Him. He wants to come to your house today and every day to spend time with you. You can talk with Him about your health, your struggles, your grandkids, your contribution to the needs of your community, and your worries about the future. Jesus will take all that you give to Him and walk with you. He will ask you to remain faithful in all things and to dwell on what is good and godly. He is making you into a new creation centered on Him, His truths, and His love. There is no greater makeover, my friend. This is the true key to living young.

1. What is interfering with your ability to meet and talk with Jesus? What hinders your closeness and personal relationship with Him?

2. What steps can you take today to cut through "the crowd," to cut through whatever is hindering you from reaching Jesus?

3. How can you stand strong in a solid Christian belief instead of a circumstantial faith?

4. What inspires your sense of hope during this season of life?

Because it is worth repeating, take a look at this list of what Paul challenges his readers to think on. As you read each line, think of something specific that represents that quality. For example, "Whatever is true" makes me think of God's Word. "Whatever is right" might bring to mind justice for the innocent. "Whatever is pure" brings up the thought of marital faithfulness. You get the idea. Here's the list to work from:

- whatever is true
- whatever is honorable
- whatever is right
- whatever is pure
- whatever is lovely
- whatever is of good repute
- whatever is excellent
- whatever is worthy of praise

PaPa Bob's Prayer

My Father in heaven, You are the source of my hope and my help. Guide me in my walk with You. Help me in my talk and my thoughts so I dwell on what matters to You. Sometimes I've felt too old to reawaken my faith, but I'm excited to know You better. God, help me draw closer to Your heart. Open my eyes to each blessing, big and small, so I will never take Your provision for granted.

Give me the boldness and desire to share my faith with my family and all the people You have intersect with my life. I want to be like Zaccheus, willing to overcome obstacles so I can spend more time with You. Amen.

❧ A Legacy Moment ❧

by *Christine Ianni* (Bob's granddaughter)

- My memories of PaPa Bob are timeless, just like he is. Whether I'm 5 or 25, PaPa always seems the same age. Even today at 80, he is as sharp and mobile as ever.

- Many years ago, he'd lead us grandkids on scavenger hunts around the yard. We'd pick flowers, cut herbs for the meal that night, collect eggs from under the chickens in the chicken coop, and pretend to fish in the pond for lean protein to add to dinner. Today PaPa could still invite us on those adventures, and we'd jump at the chance.

- I believe PaPa's longevity is the result of practicing everything in moderation. Too much of a good thing is not always a good thing, he likes to say. I too have taken that to heart.

- Papa's heart for living young wasn't developed by concentrating on physical fitness, preparing organic vegetables, or spending tons of money on vitamins and acupuncture. Instead, he wakes up and starts his day at a leisurely pace with Grammy. They spend time with the Lord and actually sing to Him in the kitchen. They enjoy home-cooked meals (that are sometimes made with organic produce mixed with expired seasonings). PaPa does make it to the gym a few times a week though.

- Papa Bob enjoys having conversations with neighbors and strangers. He reads for fun and watches his favorite sports teams play while Grammy sits nearby enjoying being with him. PaPa drives an old car and a new car.

- My grandfather's life flows beautifully. But most importantly, he is dedicated to growing God's kingdom. He's left that legacy for me and my family. We invest in many of the same things PaPa does. After all, he's the wisest man I know.

9

Legacies Are Hand-Me-Downs People Actually Want

Those who know Your name [LORD,] will put their trust in You.

Psalm 9:10

A couple of years ago, Emilie and I had the pleasure of being in Abilene, Texas, putting on a seminar. We added an extra day to drive to my birthplace, Hawley, and then continued on to my grandfather's homestead in Anson. We drove out to the farm for the first time in 45 years. As we drew near, I could feel a rush of memories welling up in my mind. I broke out in words describing all those recollections to Emilie. The buildings had long been torn down, but we took a tour of the home, the outdoor cellar, the barn, and the pastures where the livestock roamed. We took pictures to recapture the fondness of the past, and I even picked up an old brick from the home's foundation, Today it sits on my bookcase, and I often tell the story of what that brick represents.

This building block stands for so much more than a place, than a simple homestead. The brick reminds me of the place where I grew up and grew my faith. My grandfather gave me a solid grounding for my faith in God. When we often visited, we usually stayed for church. It was held in a little country church outside of town. I vividly remember Grandpa's strong voice singing the gospel hymns of old. I can still picture his eyes closed and his head bent down while in prayer.

Today families move often and roots aren't able to go as deep. We need to take the time to share with our families the strong, enduring elements of our inheritance. What has gone before us is very important to who we are today. Grandchildren love to sit on laps and go through old picture albums or scroll through photos on electronic devices. They are interested in hearing stories over and over about when they were babies.

Those who bring sunshine to the lives of others cannot keep it from themselves.
James Barrie

Live your life so when you're around others, they are uplifted and glad to be with you. Be willing to listen and provide plenty of encouragement and positive affirmations. When you spread joy, you also bring joy to your life.

Are you building an inheritance for your children and grandchildren? Will they look back and say they had a rich experience growing up? Do they know who they are? Would they recognize the pillars of your family? If not, I encourage you to pass along these timeless treasures so they can know from whence they came.

Does your family major on the minors and minor on the majors? As your time comes to be with God in heaven, have you left strong, deep tracks for those left behind to follow? Make your legacy path clear. The psalmist wrote about God, "You will make known to me the path of life; in Your presence is fullness and joy; in Your right hand there are pleasures forever" (Psalm 16:11).

Heritage matters. People need clear, steady tracks to follow. It's by divine design. We're linked to people who've
walked the long path before us. We're linked to those
who tread the trail behind. Not so very long ago, God
himself left clear human footprints in the dust of our
little world, tracks infinitely more indelible than those
left by Apollo astronauts on the airless moon. Memory
is the great encourager of spirit and life, of connectedness. And rehearsing the past is a sacred practice. It sets
the present course. It gives perspective.[1]

Grandparents have a long history of teaching their children and
grandchildren. We grandparents have great opportunities to teach
our grandchildren traditions, truths, and values their parents may
overlook or not have time for. Because of the various complexities
of today's society and family values, we can provide spiritual training when the grandchildren are with us.

What We Have to Give

Not everyone has a brick from their childhood homes, but
everyone can be a brick in the foundation of their families. There
are many ways to leave a legacy. If we look around us and don't see
land to divide among our heirs or large bank accounts to place in
trust for future generations, we still have a lot to give. Faith and
honor top the list. A great legacy is formed when we live our lives
praising God's name and when our walk with Jesus is reflected in
our talk and how we live.

Western culture doesn't give a lot of importance to the mean-
ings of our names, but bringing honor to our family names, our
Christian names, and to our family's lineage is of great value. Our
family names are so very important. We all come from a long heritage of ancestors. Some of our backgrounds we might like to sweep
under the carpet. We can't do anything about those. We all have
family members that trigger bragging rights and other ones that

almost call for apologies. Family trees have glorious limbs and ones that are rather gnarled. Even though we can't correct or change what's gone before us, we can certainly polish our present reputations. I've always emphasized to our children and grandchildren the importance of our name. Dr. J. Hamilton said,

> There is no better heritage than a good name that a father can bequeath to his children, and there are few influences on society more wholesome than the fame of its worthies.[2]

Is our name and reputation so reliable that our handshake is as good as a written contract? I remember when my grandfather did all his business with just a handshake. The tradition of the handshake came about when men approached each other and, to show they weren't carrying weapons, they extended their hands forward and open. It's a form of greeting that has extended all the way to today as a gesture of friendship.

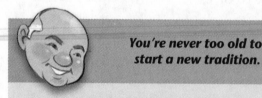

You're never too old to start a new tradition.

Don't think you're too old to start something new. Don't use your age as an excuse to not do something. God has plenty for you to do! Be open to His leading and be willing to change your routine to solidify your relationships and establish your legacy.

When They Call on Us

I call on the name of the Lord many times a day to praise Him and seek His counsel. The deep relief and comfort I feel knowing

God is with me is my built-in reminder to be a source of comfort and help for people I care about. I always direct people to God, and I always want my family and friends to know I will be a prayerful friend during their times of need. A wonderful reason to solidify our honor and faithfulness is to have names that others know they can call on when they need help.

A few years ago Emilie and I received a letter from our grandson Chad illuminating the value of being grandparents who can be called upon. Chad had just received news that his dad was going to have a biopsy to check for throat cancer. Although a serious situation, what is so wonderful is that this young man was compelled to reflect on what was most important to him during this scary time. The first half of the letter explored his gratitude for his loving parents of faith and his many other blessings. The next portion revealed his thoughts of gratitude. Emilie and I were so moved by his mature faith and his deep love for God's gift of family. We say, "Thank You, Jesus!" Here is part of Chad's letter to us:

> Dear PaPa and Grammy,
>
> PaPa and Grammy, it is because of you two that our family is as strong as we are. It is because of you guys that my two best friends in the entire world are my brother and sister, Bevan and Christine. How many kids can say that their best friends are their siblings? How many cousins talk on a normal basis and pray for each other daily? Bradley Joe says "God Bless" on his answering machine. He is twelve years old, and he is blessing God!! This is all because of you two—your faith in the Lord and your continual trust in His will.
>
> My family one day and my grandchildren one day will be amazing people, and they will be that way because of what you guys have done here on earth. I am blessed to have been born into a family of two individuals who have chosen to live their lives different from this world.

Because of your lives I was able to cry tonight for my father who I love more than I ever thought a person could love. I was able to cry to my mom at midnight because she is in daily prayer to comfort her kids. I was able to have an hour-long talk with my sister today who asked me to pray for her and who told me she loves me. I called Cousin Bradley today to see when he is going to come visit me, and I called Cousin Weston to say hello and say that I love him.

I want to end by saying happy 50-year anniversary! You two are the foundation and the stronghold of this family, and you have been for the past 50 years—and you will continue to be for the next 50 years and even as you guys depart to heaven. Because of your faithful marriage and faithful walks with Jesus, our family is able to live the lives we live and experience the love of family and the love of the Lord that we do. You guys are my heroes and my inspiration. My children and my household will be filled with the love of the Lord because of you two.

Thank you for letting me cry tonight and for allowing me to write my true feelings. PaPa, it is because of you that I write and because of you that I live for the Lord. PaPa and Grammy, I love you.

Your grandson,
Chad

GOD'S "LIVING YOUNG" WISDOM

Have you ever been challenged regarding what kind of legacy you are leaving for your heirs? We all leave behind the evidences of our belief system. It will either be good and positive or it will be bad and negative. Either way, it will have an impact on our heirs.

Paul writes to his friend Timothy and challenges him to remember the influence that his mother and grandmother had upon his life. The apostle encourages Timothy to concentrate on the past, present, and future aspects of developing a legacy. Paul wants his friend to "fan the flame" of his faith for God.

The second part of the legacy was to follow the plan that God had given them. The character development Timothy needed to embrace and live out was that God had not given him a spirit of timidity (cowardice) but one of power, love, and discipline. Paul warned him that at times he might have to suffer for preaching the gospel. He stressed not to be ashamed, but to believe and be convinced that Jesus would guard what had been entrusted to Him (2 Timothy 1:3-18).

Another aspect of passing this legacy to others is to pattern our lives from what we have seen. Paul stressed that we retain the standard of sound words that we have heard from him. We are to guard, through the Holy Spirit, the treasure (gospel) that has been entrusted to us.

The last aspect of developing a worthwhile legacy is to pass it on. Paul told Timothy to entrust these truths to "faithful men who will be able to teach others also" (2 Timothy 2:2). God wants us to be men who care about the legacy we will leave when the Lord calls us home. We are to teach our children these truths too:

- Fan the flame of passion for God.
- Follow God's plan for you.
- Pattern your life from what you have learned [from Jesus].
- Pass [your faith and wisdom] on to those who will follow.[3]

You and I have the incredible opportunity to leave behind legacies of care and concern that reach out to people with generosity and a sharing of God's holiness. We want to be the kind of men who care about the people left behind when the Lord calls us home. And for those of us who don't have kids or grandkids, we need to not think for a second that building a legacy isn't important. The way we live has great value and will have an impact for God on future generations.

Traditions and Celebrations

Traditions and celebrations allow the zest for life to be passed from generation to generation. They have filled our lives with many beautiful treasures over the years, providing memories we share and laugh, smile, and have tears of joys over. We want to pass these treasures and the creation of new ones on to our children and grandchildren. How do we do this? By sharing and celebrating our special ways of doing things, many of which have been passed down through the generations in our families.

Yes, traditions add joy and richness to our lives, but that doesn't mean all traditions have to be continued. As our grown kids have children and begin their own traditions, it is important to be flexible and allow them to create their own traditions or update our family traditions. This is especially important when our children and grandchildren marry because they'll need to incorporate some of their loved ones' traditions into their lives. This can be a wonderful time to evaluate traditions and keep the ones that enhance our families and modify or eliminate the ones that don't quite fit anymore. In a way, traditions are like closets. If we keep adding new ones and never give up old ones, we'll end up with overstuffed lives, halfhearted observances, and too much stress from trying to do too much. But when we keep our priorities straight, our ideas flexible, and our desires to celebrate each other and our families upbeat, strong traditions will enhance everyone's life and create memories that help bind family members together.

Ring in the Season

We need to look forward to the future, planning for making memories and establishing new traditions that will draw our families together for years to come. After all, the memories of tomorrow are being shaped by the traditions we create today.

Emilie and I have had such fun establishing traditions in our family. One of the most meaningful began during our first Christmas together. Money was tight that year, but we managed to get a tree and we gave each other ornaments as gifts. And we've continued to give each other ornaments through our many years together. When the children were born, they got ornaments too. Years later, when Jenny got married at age 22, we gave Jenny and her husband the "Jenny" ornaments to adorn their first tree.

And the tradition continues as our family grows. Some years ago we decided not to give ornaments; after 33 years we thought nobody cared. How wrong we were! Everybody was so disappointed that we went out first thing on December 26 and found just the right ornaments to continue the tradition. The practice of giving ornaments still warms everyone's heart when we gather together.

And if our children and grandchildren live far away, why not send them their ornaments around the end of November? That way they'll have them to put on their tree. And over the years, they'll look forward to the arrival of the package that carries ornament treasures from the grandparents.

Easy Celebration Ideas

Every season of the year brings with it possibilities for gathering, honoring one another, and extending love and hospitality to family and friends. Taking a glance at a year's worth of seasons and reasons to enjoy each other increases our gratitude for the lives God has blessed us with.

And remember, celebrations and activities don't have to include spending a lot of money. Ignore the hype of commercialism and embrace a healthy attitude toward your celebrations. Holidays should give us something to look forward to! Don't let them become cause for financial stress. That's the consumer mindset. Let that perspective go and become a person who shows others how holidays and gatherings can be opportunities to share love, rest, and refreshments. If we view these times as chances to take a break from routine, they can be seasons of delight rather than seasons full of demands and pressures.

Here's a quick look over the year's calendar with some opportunities for joyful celebrations.

One fun way to ring in the New Year is to set aside a day for food and games. Ask those who received games for Christmas to bring them. Then divide into groups to play them. One family I know developed a New Year's Eve tradition of playing games until midnight. At that point, they stopped and welcomed the beginning of the new year.

Valentine's Day is packed with possibilities for celebrating the special people in your life. Treat your young grandchildren to a Valentine's Day cookie-making or birdhouse-making activity so their parents can have a date night. Everyone wins!

Spring is perfect for flying kites, riding bikes, throwing Frisbees, and enjoying picnics. Have the whole family host a garage sale, and when you're through, use some of the proceeds to celebrate with pizza or ice cream.

If your church celebrates Ash Wednesday, Maundy Thursday, Good Friday, and Easter—make a commitment to attend all the services together. Or you can enrich your understanding of God's family by attending services at a church with different traditions than you're used to.

Summer is a great time to celebrate. Take everyone fishing, swimming, or rock climbing. Have hot dog roasts, volleyball games, or croquet competitions. If you live near the coast, hold a neighborhood clambake. If you don't, then pretend by throwing a clam-chowder party.

The Fourth of July and Labor Day provide wonderful, festive opportunities for outdoor celebrations. Why not throw a block party? Close off the street (if possible) and ask the neighbors to bring cold cuts, watermelon, ice cream, and other warm-weather goodies. Let the neighbor children decorate their bikes, little cars, ponies, dogs, and participate in a neighborhood parade.

Autumn brings golden days that call out for celebrations. If you have a garden, rediscover an old tradition and invite friends and family over to help you harvest. Afterward everyone can enjoy some of the bounty harvested.

Halloween, with its pagan history, is problematic for many Christians. But children and adults love the fun of dressing up in costumes and playing games, so why not provide a safe, festive, Christ-centered alternative on October 31 or another time in the year? Perhaps you can establish a yearly costume party to celebrate a birthday, anniversary, holiday, or retirement. Or celebrate All Saints Day on the first of November by dressing up as biblical people or great Christians of the past.

Thanksgiving is a wonderful time for celebrating the gifts God has given us. Don't waste it by just stuffing down food. Attend special Thanksgiving services or, even better, have one of your own. For almost 20 years, Emilie and I hosted a Thanksgiving service in our home for family, friends, neighbors, and anyone else who wanted to come. It started when we decided to begin the day by giving thanks to God. When the children got a bit older, they wanted to invite their friends. Their parents were intrigued and wanted to come too. Emilie and I served hot cider and cinnamon rolls. As the tradition grew, others brought goodies to eat. Our service begins with a time of singing, and then people share what they are thankful for. What a beautiful hour we experience even as pain and joy are shared. Our service has become a beautiful tradition filled with heart, love, and the spirit of celebration.

And then comes Christmas. There is so much we can do to celebrate without losing touch with the real cause for celebration—the birth on earth of our Lord and Savior, Jesus Christ.

The Barnes family has a tradition of reading one new book every Christmas. It could be a Christmas story or an Easter story. Other families read the same story every year. Check with your Christian bookstore for a family book of stories.

Involve the whole family in your celebrations. One way to do this is to involve the children in a play or let them perform some other way. Last year at our family Christmas party, one child recited from Luke while the other children acted out the story. Many of us blinked back tears as we watched the children in their makeshift costumes telling the story of Jesus' birth.

You can designate one person to be the picture-taker or have multiple cameras available. At the end of the celebration or within a week or so, transfer the pictures to CDs and pass them out or send them to everyone who came to the party. You'll have great fun talking about the photos and the memories they bring up. Each Christmas we also set aside time to have a family photo taken.

YOUR GUIDE TO LIVING YOUNG

Live young and live with conviction as a man who knows the value of a good name, solid reputation, and an authentic faith walk with Jesus. Don't live life with an ounce of stinginess, anger, and regret. Instead, live with an open heart and a willingness to share your wisdom, advice, kindness, and time. Be ready with a listening ear, asking if the person sharing wants advice or just support.

Give to your family, your friends, your coworkers, your community, and your world by giving of yourself without expecting something in return. If you weigh how much you give and compare that to how much you receive, you won't understand or receive the full blessings God wants you to experience in this season of life.

Do you remember those "I was caught being good" stickers I mentioned in an earlier chapter? Think about how you share your legacy. Would God regularly give you one of those stickers?

1. In what kind of condition are your life hand-me-downs? Is the way you live your life something your heirs and others will want to try on?

2. Does your name have honor? Do you keep your word to your family, friends, and acquaintances?

3. How are you currently sharing your legacy of faith? What can you do to share even more?

4. What traditions have you held on to that, perhaps, should be changed or let go of? What are your ideas for new traditions?

PaPa Bob's Prayer

Lord, preserve in me the desire to be a man of my word. Forgive me for the times when I hold back from giving to others because I lack confidence or because I'm worried that I won't get enough of something in return.

Help me participate fully in family celebrations. Give me the desire to invest in making memories and building a foundation of family time together.

Father, I hope You catch me doing good time after time. Keep me open to Your guidance in every circumstance and in every moment. Every "right now" is part of Your eternity. May I share Your legacy of love with a devoted, fervent heart. Amen.

10

Aim to Connect by Shooting the Breeze

In the fear of the LORD there is strong confidence,
and his children will have refuge.

Proverbs 14:26

As a family growing up on a farm in central Texas, we had on phone that hung on a wall. It was the old-fashioned kind with a crank. We shared a "party line" with up to four other families. We each had a distinct ring so we'd know who was being called. Today people have smart phones, laptops, tablets, notebooks, and a myriad of other electronic gadgets to keep in touch. In the old days when we called someone and got a busy signal, we'd have to hang up and redial. Not today. We just keep pushing the redial button, and it keeps ringing over and over until we get through. Or we can push another button, go about our business, and when the person picks up, our phone will ring us back!

Busy signals are a thing of the past, but often we keep sending them out to our younger family members and friends—sometimes on purpose, but most often inadvertently. How do we do this? By our attitudes and our own busyness. Even if our attention is not taken over by a technological wonder device, our attention to anything other than the young person wanting to talk to us is, by far, a more damaging busy signal than what our old phones used to give us. Our inattention says to the young person (or our spouses or our other loved ones) they are not of sufficient value to override what we're focused on…that we have more important things to do than listen to them or be with them in mind and spirit.

When Busy Signals Become SOS Signals

I have a friend who doesn't have grandchildren, but she has nephews. She told me about something that her eldest nephew used to do when he was five or so. He would go up to talk to someone. If the person was doing something else and mumbling responses to him, her little nephew would reach out and gently turn the person's face toward him. Although very cute, it was also humbling to realize that to get the attention he desired (and perhaps needed), he had to physically ask for it.

Yes, the most destructive busy signals occur right in our homes. Busy signals go something like this:

- "Not now but maybe later."
- "Wait until I finish the paper."
- "Can't you find something else to do?"
- "Ask your grandmother or your parents."
- "Your grandpa is too tired right now."

Happiness can be achieved by using your patience.

Those who are patient win the race of life. Impatient people create a lot of physical ailments because of the stress they cause for themselves and others. People love to be around patient people, and they shy away from those who are impatient.

Busy signals become SOS signals when they cause us to ignore, delay, dismiss, or even degrade our grandchildren's need for our attention. And if we initiate ways to keep the child busy so he or she won't "bother" us, the same obstacle to communication exists. Have you noticed how quick many parents and grandparents are to place a child in front of a television, computer, smart phone, or tablet? These high-tech, low-cost nannies take the place of what could be one-on-one time between that child and a loving, listening adult. Too many grandpas have yielded to the temptation to buy off their grandchildren with money, things, and organized activities. They keep them distracted or entertained instead of taking the time to talk and interact with them. Yes, sometimes it can be hard to get kids to talk to us adults, but that doesn't mean we should give up. I've discovered that we men tend to communicate better while doing something, so engage in an activity with your grandchildren that keeps you close enough for communication, such as hiking, fishing, or putting a jigsaw puzzle together.

When David called upon his heavenly Father there were no busy signals. God did not tell David to go stare at the sheep and leave Him alone or wait there until He arrived. God was present to David and listened to him whether it was night or day. Many psalms reflect David's awareness that God could be reached and communicated with always. That, along with knowing God's great love for him, was David's greatest source of comfort.

- The Lord has set apart the godly man for Himself; the Lord hears when I call to Him (Psalm 4:3).

- Give ear to my words, O Lord, consider my groaning (5:1).

- O Lord my God, in You I have taken refuge (7:1).

- You, O Lord, have not forsaken those who seek You (9:10).

God has an open ear to even our faintest cry. Isn't that a great example for us? It's an encouragement to spend quality and quantity time with our grandchildren, to be an approachable man, never too busy to hear small or large things. As a dad I learned that communication was much better when I started the process early in my children and grandchildren's lives so it became a regular, expected part of our relationship. Times of sincere listening and talking meant each child knew I was available to talk anytime they'd like. They also knew I would seek them out for conversations about life, faith, their interests, and my interests. Listening to my children from the very beginning of their days, from baby coos to funny conversations, has made my life richer, more fulfilling, and joyful.

So long as we love, we serve; so long as we are loved by others, I should say that we are almost indispensable; and no man is useless while he has a friend.

Robert Louis Stevenson

Necessity is the beginning of invention. When God closes one door, He opens another. During this season of your life, make yourself useful by opening your heart and ears to the people around you.

Emilie and I had a good friend who was a professional man. He wasn't accustomed to working in dirt or grease. He felt he was losing connection with his teenage son who had recently gotten involved in motorbikes. This father went to his pastor and asked, "What shall I do?" The pastor told him to spend time by his son's side and become interested in motorbikes. "But, pastor, I don't like dirt and grease!" the man responded. The pastor replied, "I thought you wanted to make contact with your son?" So Dad rolled up his sleeves and got dirty. When the boy grew up, this dad and son ended up partnering in a service station that pumps gas and does vehicle smog checks and repairs. This was a father who realized he needed to get involved with his teenage son to stay connected and maintain a relationship.

God's "Living Young" Wisdom

By today's standards, life when I was growing up moved at a snail's pace. Looking back it seems so old-fashioned. What we wore as bathing suits was unbelievable. Couples didn't live together before they were married. Ladies couldn't wear white wedding gowns at their wedding unless they had remained pure while dating. Men and women didn't kiss on the first date. Most people wouldn't want to return to the "good old days" because life was hard and money was tight, but the positive was that many of the moral values were based on God's Word. More than 2500 years ago, God's prophet Jeremiah reminded people that there is nothing more up-to-date than the truth of the past. "Stand by the ways and see and ask for the ancient paths, where the good way is, and walk in it; and you will find rest for your souls" (Jeremiah 6:16). Even though Jeremiah was regarded as old-fashioned and out-of-date at the time, he urged his family and friends to walk in the old paths of truth so they would find peace for their souls.

Jesus gives us a similar promise:

> Come to Me, all who are weary and heavy-laden, and I will give you rest. Take My yoke upon you and learn from Me, for I am gentle and humble in heart; and YOU WILL FIND REST FOR YOUR SOULS. For My yoke is easy and My burden is light (Matthew 11:28-30).

This great invitation, extended to everyone, is threefold:

- come to Jesus to receive salvation
- learn in discipleship with Him
- serve in tandem with the Lord

The yoke involves instruction under discipline. Yet Jesus promises that learning with Him will be much easier than trying to follow the law as the Jews did. Today rest and peace in Jesus is still available to everyone who will accept Him as Lord and Savior.

We Are Valuable Educators

After college I spent 14 years in the education field. It was a very exciting time of my life. I look back on those early years and still remember the names of many of my students. Among my favorite annual events were the back-to-school nights. It was such a fun evening. I remember telling parents, "I won't believe everything your children tell me about you if you won't believe everything they tell you about me." I always enjoyed the person-to-person interactions during those evenings and throughout the school year.

Parental involvement has a greater influence on children's success in school and life than the quality of teachers, the school, and the money spent on education. And now, many years later, I firmly believe a grandparent's influence in these areas can also be of great significance.

Children achieve in many arenas when parents and other adults read to them, when mentors value them, and when adults make family time together a priority. Are such interactions important to you? If the spiritual and emotional education of your grandchild and other young people is important to you, the following bits of wisdom will help you be a positive influence.

No matter how busy you are, make the sacrifice of time to enhance and strengthen children for their future. Grandparents can project a positive attitude by letting children know they are special. Recognize and let each child know he or she is an individual worth knowing. Avoid comparing children with other children. Concentrate on the positives and recognize a child's efforts, not just the result or accomplishment.

Treat children with as much respect as you treat adults. Children know when they are respected by a grandparent, parent, teacher, and mentor. If they feel heard, they are more likely to open up and communicate about their lives, including the hard times they face.

Listen to children carefully. Avoid telling them they are bad or they are good. By that I mean we should listen to what they say and then be careful to address only specifics. Don't make general "you are good" or "you are bad" statements. Instead, praise or correct specific behaviors. Effective praise tells the child, "I like how you helped Johnnie with his homework" or "I am pleased you did so well on your spelling test." Effective discipline is also specific and tells a child "I like you, but I disagree with your behavior." For example, "I don't like how you were rude to your friend on the phone."

Discourage children from putting themselves or others down. Negative words, even when allegedly said in jest or with sarcasm, create animosity between siblings, peers, and generations. It sets the stage for children and adults to start believing the negative talk. Just because we adults are older and wiser doesn't mean we aren't capable of being hurt by what is said. Don't allow criticism and sarcasm to become part of your grandchildren's attitudes and language. These traits hurt the person on the receiving end of the insensitive comment and can impact the entire family or group. Your positive self-talk and positive talking with others can be great examples for your grandchildren. You are modeling God's love and grace.

Be the role model you want your grandchildren to have. To have your grandchildren be open to spending time with you so you can be a role model, start with a "shooting the breeze" session. First get past your worry that you might not be able to relate to your grandchildren. They need you, and they want the attention you give them even if they don't always show it. We can't expect children to model kindness if they never receive it. We can't challenge children to learn and grow if they don't see our willingness to learn and grow. We can show them education matters by sharing about our favorite subjects when we were their ages and inviting them to tell us about their school lessons, their favorite studies, and what subjects give them trouble. Then we can extend the discussion into other areas of growth, including spirituality and social situations.

Train Up a Child

Wouldn't it be wonderful if we could send some children to something akin to dog obedience training? (I mean *other* children—not your family's offspring because they're perfect or almost perfect, right?) My youngest grandchild recently sent their family's hyperactive pup to a dog trainer. This dog was a nutcase. It was constantly jumping up, digging, and exhibiting poor manners. For this dog to fit in with the family, it had to be sent to someone who could and would teach it proper behavior. Otherwise, they were going to have to find this dog a new home.

After five weeks and several hundred dollars, the pup returned to their home a well-behaved dog. All its negatives had been reduced to zero or close to it. This trainer was a miracle-worker! Now people can visit my grandchild's home and not be greeted with dirty paws on their chests.

Okay, so we can't really send children to obedience training, but we can take seriously our duties as teachers and mentors. And, if you don't have grandchildren, I'm sure there are children you can be involved with at church, in children's sports, or at schools. We are all responsible to connect with and help the next generation. We want to give them something positive.

If you're not sure how you can help train up a child, start with the very heart of any relationship: good communication. We can teach children the art of conversation. Yes, it is learned behavior. First, find ways to interact with younger generations. There are many open doors through church and community activities. You could attend area high school sport and drama events. Talk to the kids about the areas they're passionate about. If you still own or work with a business, see if your company will sponsor a sport's team and then cheer that team on at the games. Show your support and care by talking to the kids and their parents. Be present and attentive to others because your availability is what makes impromptu talks possible, and that's the beginning of many relationships. We help train people in the art of communication by inviting them to converse with us.

And bear in mind that the need for conversation isn't limited to our teen and preteen population. People of every age need interaction. Many middle-aged men would also benefit greatly from having an older man to talk to about faith, recreation, relationships, and other issues. If they are all about work or striving to be successful, your conversations could help them explore the importance of other areas, including spiritual health and familial priorities.

A New SOS

If you engage a child in conversation and seem to be getting nowhere, instead of sending up a flare of distress, why not shift to another kind of SOS? I'm talking about "Share Your Story." Sharing about your experiences helps create a common ground with children. Even if your background, hometown, and personal interests are very different from their own, they'll appreciate knowing you also had "first day of school" jitters, or a crush on the girl next door, or a time when you were overcome with embarrassment.

When I visit with my grandchildren, they like to ask me about the "good old days." What was it like waaaay back then? They can't believe a gallon of gas was 33 cents, everyone didn't own a phone, and computers weren't available to the general public. They ask how we ever got anything done and whether we ever had any fun.

Do you know what's so exciting about the legacy of memories? Memories require an investment of ourselves. When we share personal memories, we're revealing a part of our lives. And we're creating a memory by interacting, communicating, and relating stories that reveal how we became who we are and that we're real people who experienced real events and have something to share. Each event of your life provides a powerful opportunity to share and develop a stronger, more intimate relationship with another generation. Never hold back the urge to share a story from the past. They are building blocks for future generations. They help create a foundation of life experiences to draw from.

Often when I feel a little melancholy I think back a few years (okay, even decades) and recall the history-making moments in my life. One of my strongest memories came about when I was nine years old. Our family had just moved from New Mexico to Long Beach, California. It was 1942, and American involvement in World War II had just started. A new job for Dad at a starting wage, expenses from moving, and general family expenses had a negative impact on our lives. Mom and Dad told us kids there wouldn't be any extra money for Christmas that year. My two brothers and I didn't like hearing those words because we were just kids, but we understood the situation. On Christmas morning we had no gifts under our small Christmas tree. About midday we looked out the living room window and eyed our uncle who was walking up to the front door. In his hand he had three wrapped packages. We were excited because we hoped they were for us... and they were! We were so thrilled to each get a gift.

Many Christmases have come and gone since then, but none

match the thrill of that morning. As I hurriedly tore open the wrapping, my eyes and fingers realized what was inside—a bow and arrow! The arrows had rubber suction cups on the ends. That gift stands out as the best gift I've ever received on Christmas morning because I'd believed I wouldn't be getting a present.

I'm sure you have similar stories to be told. Each story represents our heritage of love, worldview, and family values. They tell a story that is certainly worth sharing!

What Young'uns Long For

In a paper my grandson Chad wrote about his high school days, he shared a perspective that might come as a surprise to many people. I think you'll be surprised too!

> Most men don't realize that young men in their late teens to early 20s need older men to encourage and mentor us. Without this, we will become weak. Most men don't realize how important they are in the lives of future generations.
>
> My PaPa Bob has made it a priority to teach younger men the lessons he has learned. PaPa has participated in a variety (hundreds probably) of conversations with my friends on a wide range of topics. I have had friends in high school and college take Friday nights to drive to Orange County just to speak with PaPa Bob. PaPa said he never understood why such good-looking guys would want to hang out with an older man on a Friday night when he knew all of the good-looking ladies his grandson attracted. The truth was that my friends and I legitimately did get more out of learning from PaPa than we would have from partying. Every time we left PaPa's house we were encouraged to be more.
>
> A friend and I once said if we could be half the man PaPa was, we would be successful in life as husbands, friends,

and businessmen. We truly grew from his conversations. The funniest part is he thought we were weird for wanting to hang with him, but we thought he was weird for wanting to hang with boring high school kids.

Yes, Chad and his friends enjoyed spending time with their old grandpa. The real surprise is the revelation that young men want to be around godly men who are willing to share their wisdom and take the time to listen to their thoughts and questions about life.

My motivation for being available to Chad and his many friends was to share Christ with these youngsters. Scripture provides many verses that stress togetherness. These might encourage you to build a legacy by encouraging and serving others.

- Let no one seek his own good, but that of his neighbor (1 Corinthians 10:24).

- Through love serve one another (Galatians 5:13).

- Be kind to one another, tender-hearted, forgiving each other (Ephesians 4:32).

- Teach and admonish one another (Colossians 3:16 NIV).

- Encourage one another (1 Thessalonians 5:11).

- Spur one another on toward love and good deeds (Hebrews 10:24 NIV).

- Pray for one another (James 5:16).

- Offer hospitality to one another without grumbling (1 Peter 4:9 NIV).

- Have fellowship with one another (1 John 1:7).

We need to pattern our lives after what we've learned through the Scriptures. We want to be men of character and principles so we can pass on an honorable, helpful legacy.

Conversation Starters

If diving right into conversations is not your style, watch for ways to engage in casual discussions during everyday moments. You might be surprised what can become an ongoing conversation piece. Years ago my young grandson Weston proudly gave me a medium-sized beige canvas bag with a drawstring at the top. The words PaPa's Bag were scrawled across the front in brightly colored ink and the charming penmanship of a four-year-old. Weston informed me this bag was to be filled with all kinds of goodies and placed in the backseat of our van. Little morsels of nutrition and other treats were to be in the bag so they'd be available when the kids got into my car. (Not only kids wanted PaPa's bag filled and ready for them. Adults also want to share in "PaPa's Bag.")

This bag was a great conversation starter between my grandchildren and me. On occasion they informed me, "PaPa, you need to fill up your bag with better stuff. It's not too good now." I'd laugh and start a discussion on what constituted better. Later I'd head off to the market to fill "PaPa's Bag" with better stuff.

Picture This

You've heard the saying that a picture is worth a thousand words, right? Well, I suggest a picture also can inspire a thousand words of great conversation. And what better way to start a conversation than looking at photographs! Isn't it fun to look through old albums and recall the special events of your life? I believe the photograph is truly one of the greatest inventions of all time. They help us remember past holidays, weddings, celebrations, graduations, and every other grand occasion we've experienced. When we share photos with younger people, we can ask all sorts of questions to get the conversation rolling:

- What was going on when this photo was taken?
- How were you feeling that day?

- Describe what you enjoyed most about that vacation.
- What do you remember about this event that isn't shown in the photo?

Another way to pass along your love and values to your children is to share special mementos. When our children, Jenny and Brad, graduated from high school, Emilie and I prepared a "This Is Your Life" album for each of them. We bought scrapbooks and decorated the covers. We filled them with items from their lives, from birth announcements to graduation pictures. There were report cards, hand-drawn pictures they did when they were young, invitations to parties, photos of friends, and letters they'd written to us from summer camp. Even now Jenny and Brad refer to their scrapbooks to help them remember names and important dates. They entertain their children with this evidence that they too were once young!

Many conversations will be initiated via those albums. They give Jenny and Brad opportunities to pass along their legacies to the next generation. Future generations will also be able to get a glimpse of their family history and heritage through those albums. Just reminiscing about the albums sparks conversations between Emilie and me.

I love this quote from author and pastor Stu Weber: "Memory is the great encourager of spirit and life, of connectedness. And rehearsing the past is a sacred practice. It sets the present course. It gives perspective." Sharing memories and making new ones creates opportunities for conversations with the people in your life, young and old. Be open to impromptu talks that may arise during everyday activities. These can set the tone for many talks to come.

YOUR GUIDE TO LIVING YOUNG

Shy ones, bold ones, sad ones, happy ones…every young person will blossom beneath the warmth of times you spend with him sharing your wisdom and your thoughtful, listening spirit. Show young men how much their opinions and questions count by inviting them to share with you about their lives. Welcome any questions they may have about life, specific situations, and relationships.

Do you know who else could probably use someone who will listen, share, and provide advice? Fathers of young men. Watch for and then step up for opportunities to share with dads in their 30s, 40s, and 50s. You can offer biblical wisdom and your experiences on parenting, marriage, and balancing work and family. If you received such a gift from an older man, draw from that experience to share. If you never received support from older men, let that loss be your motivation to make a positive difference in a man's life.

1. When have you given someone a busy signal because you felt too busy to pay attention?

2. What barriers keep you from being a good communicator? Ask God for help in your weak areas. Consider whether you lack patience, willingness, confidence, or boldness.

3. Take time to thank God for each man who took time to listen to you and ask about your life when you were growing up.

Step out in faith and share your story. What's the value of having more history than others if you don't share the good, the bad, and the amazing?

PaPa Bob's Prayer

Father God, when I hold back from sharing with a younger person, release my worries and reveal the best way to enter into conversation. Open my heart and my ears at the same time so I will be a thoughtful listener and a discerning man of faith in You. Fill me with curiosity and appreciation as I invite other generations to share their interests and concerns. Remind me what it feels like to be young. Bring to my mind all the ways You guided me and inspired me through the timely comments, advice, and concern of godly men in my lifetime. Then help me do the same. Amen.

❧ A Legacy Moment ❧

by *Patrick Ianni* (Bob's grandson-in-law)

Characteristics of My Young-at-Heart PaPa Bob

- Guy's guy
- Sharp dresser
- Loves conversation
- Unselfish
- Captain of hope
- General of generosity
- Sports enthusiast
- Silver-lining finder
- Involved and supportive grandfather

Keep On Keeping On

Fixing our eyes on Jesus the author and perfecter of faith.

Hebrews 12:2

I look forward to watching the Olympics every four years to enjoy the prowess of the most gifted, well-trained, disciplined athletes in the world. Whether the challenge before the athlete is a 50-meter freestyle swim or a 26-mile marathon, the goal is the same: to finish and finish well. They've prepared for years through grueling training and dedicated mental focus. Many have left home, family, and other comforts to immerse themselves in the world of strict routine, faithful workouts, and perseverance

When athletes finish their chosen events, their hearts are pounding and they are fully exhausted because of lack of oxygen from the severe effort to win. Was the effort worth all the sacrifices they made? I'm sure every one of them would say yes. In fact, even the ones who don't earn a medal are usually planning what changes to make in their training before the next Olympics. They've learned to always look toward their goals. And that's the way believers must approach life too.

> The law of nature is that a certain quantity of work is necessary to produce a certain quantity of good of any kind whatever. If you want knowledge, you must toil

for it; if food, you must toil for it; and if pleasure, you must toil for it (John Ruskin).

The writer of the book of Hebrews tells us that we are to "run with endurance the race that is set before us" (12:1). And just because you and I have quite a few years under our belts doesn't mean we can drop out. We are still in the race, my friend. We don't know how the future will play out, but we do know the One who holds the future. "[Jesus'] divine power has given us everything we need for a godly life through our knowledge of him who called us by his own glory and goodness. Through these he has given us his very great and precious promises, so that through them you may participate in the divine nature" (2 Peter 1:3-4). Even when we're feeling down, we haven't lost hope. Our faith in our wonderful Creator gives us the strength to live another day with hope and verve based in Him.

We aren't in a competition or battle, but we're called to do our best in this race called life. The destination does matter, and so does the way we press on when people in the world might tell us to drop out or question why we're still keeping on the course we've chosen. We need to ignore those voices and, instead, seek God's blessing, approval, and guidance.

When life circumstances aren't going like we want them to, we can look to God for strength and encouragement. We can read again His promises given to us in His Word. We can stand in God's presence and receive a deep, lasting hope, amazing comfort, and an awesome peace. Because of His grace, we have abundant life to look forward to. God's promises give us what we need for this very moment and for all eternity.

Joy in the Journey

The idea of enjoying the journey of life is expressed pretty frequently in our culture. That message isn't new. Sadly, many people have heard that comment and then thought, "That's for other people. I have *real* life to worry about and deal with." But let's stop and take a look at what those people are missing by holding on to that attitude. They are choosing to live without joy. God doesn't want anyone to experience a joyless life journey. If we interpret Christian perseverance as drudgery, then we are missing out on the power and passion of perseverance. God wants us to receive joy from His blessings and His challenges for us.

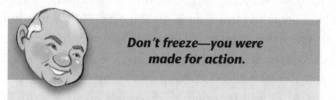

Don't freeze—you were made for action.

Don't let doubt hold you back. God wants to keep you moving forward in His purpose for you. Just keep stepping out in faith. If you stay in communication with Him, when you get off track, He'll guide you back to His path.

Life can be boring or exciting, depending on which attitude and view we choose to take. I recommend taking time to evaluate your purposes in life. I've found that men who write out their "mission goals" and look to the future seem to have a greater excitement for life. Those who have never thought out what life is all about and only live for the moment seem to get quickly bored. Nothing satisfies a restless soul.

My formula for experiencing a happy life is to live with purpose. Give yourself away to a cause. Andrew Murray said it so well: "I have learned to place myself before God every day as a vessel to be filled with His Holy Spirit. He has given me the blessed assurance that He, as the everlasting God, has guaranteed His own work in me." Some of us are called to labor by plowing or planting or harvesting. Each one of us has a special calling given by God to accomplish His purposes. I pray we will all grasp the excitement of living life for God. One key to realizing what gifts and talents God has given us is to recognize what we enjoy doing. That usually indicates our areas of interest. We need to do what we like to do for the Lord with all the energy and creativity we have. No matter what our calling, it has great value regardless of any social ranking or prestige the world may apply to our line of service.

David wrote, "Delight yourself in the LORD; and He will give you the desires of your heart. Commit your way to the LORD, trust also in Him, and He will do it" (Psalm 37:4-5). Two words stand out to me in this passage: "delight" and "commit." These are action words that require us to think and plan. We want to live life with purpose not by accident. We can take control of our lives, so we don't need to wait for others to determine our fate. With God's help, we will experience complete enjoyment and rise each morning with songs in our hearts and bounce in our walk. In fact, people will stand back and ask us, "What's come over you? There's something different about you today!"

Don't focus on fairness; focus on faith.

In today's world bad things seem to happen to good people, and often bad people seem to get rewarded. Don't worry or be concerned because God is in charge. Your faith in Him will move you forward and be your reward.

Laughter in the Walls

As seniors, we have the pleasure of thinking back to all the fun we've had in our lives. It's amazing how many celebrations are carried forward to the following generations. We can choose to live

in isolation or we can go the extra mile and bring the next generation into our celebrations.

I've so enjoyed the events I've shared in this book—the good
and the bad. The many struggles, victories, and long stretches of
status quo that have made up my lifetime provided variety, growth,
and interest. These times all link together to form my history, my
path, my legacy.

I'm grateful to be here right now too. I'm thankful that I get
to delight in the joys Emilie and I have experienced in our marriage, in raising a family, in serving through ministry, and in day-
to-day living. I even appreciate the laughter and tears we've shared
through Emilie's medical journey battling cancer because those
sweet and bittersweet moments have drawn us closer together and
closer to God. What great gifts God has bestowed!

Each leg of my life trip has taught me the lessons I needed to
serve God to the best of my ability and be where I am today. Do
you believe that for your life too? We all have experiences in our
lives that seemed like trouble at the time but were actually opportunities to draw closer to someone and to God. Most of us have
those circumstances happen regularly. Even a normal, hard-to-get-
out-of-bed Monday can be a reason to draw close to God's heart
and seek His joy for the day.

I believe laughter is a definite component of many "memory
moments" our families will cherish. Humor is a gift from God that
brightens our good times and lightens the shadows when we walk
in the dark valleys of life. Laughter even has a healing quality to it.
Smiling and laughing will bring joy and healing to your body and
soul if you allow it.

I firmly believe people have recovered from serious illnesses by
learning to find humor in each day. This life skill empowers people to go on and face painful circumstances with courage. When
Emilie was going through chemotherapy and radiation for cancer,
her doctors told us that a positive attitude and mindset had a great

deal to do with the potential for healing. When our attitudes are honed with love and joy, we are stronger and more able to pierce the clouds of depression and sickness.

Laughter also draws people to us, and as we share, we help lighten their loads and they lighten ours. We see a promising speck of light at the end of the tunnel. I enjoy telling humorous stories and jokes (at least I think they're funny). Here's one to make you smile:

> A newspaper reporter went to interview a woman who was celebrating being 102 years old. He asked, "What was the most difficult time of your life?" She thought for a moment and replied, "The second hundred years is harder than the first hundred."

When talking with my grandchildren by phone, I always try to share a joke. Since I'm not funny by nature, I keep a joke book near the phone so I can open it and reel off a few funnies. And over the years, whenever I write someone a note, I insert a few chuckle-producing stories or quips.

When my granddaughter Christine was seven years old, she called me up and told me a joke. That began a long tradition of the two of us telling each other jokes when we speak in person or on the phone. The enjoyment of simple, clean humor brightens our day, and our laughter and humor often makes those around us laugh too. I encourage you to discover the joy of laughter. Look for something each day that makes you smile or laugh out loud.

GOD'S "LIVING YOUNG" WISDOM

The word "love" is used so loosely today. We love our pets, but that's different than loving our mates. We love a piece of music, a cool breeze on a hot afternoon, and a tricked-out car. We love our children, families, and close friends. We say we love our jobs (hopefully) and our favorite foods. Falling in love is surely different from those types of loves.

Learning more about "love" will help us understand how it can start out as a "like" and progress to the point where both people desire to make a lifetime commitment to each other. Most of us know from experience that the "feeling of being in love" can be misleading and even fade away. Emilie and I went to my fiftieth high school reunion. As we were driving home, I commented, "I'm certainly glad I didn't marry the girls I had that love feeling for in high school." I guess that's one advantage of going back to school reunions. We realize that God had a better plan for our lives!

Individuals who make decisions solely based on their feelings are usually unstable in several areas. But when love is based on more than feelings, it can be a rock-solid foundation. Scripture provides a very clear definition of what real love, biblical love, is all about. First Corinthians 13:4-7 is probably the most cited Scripture in wedding ceremonies:

> Love is patient, love is kind. It does not envy, it does not boast, it is not proud. It does not dishonor others, it is not self-seeking, it is not easily angered, it keeps no record of wrongs. Love does not delight in evil but rejoices with the truth. It always protects, always trusts, always hopes, always perseveres (NIV).

Love is more than a childish emotion. It's much greater than the worldly love portrayed in romantic novels, television shows, and movies. It's deeper than the feelings we have for our close friends. Often this "real" love results in marriages. That's why many pastors and counselors recommend that courtship should last a minimum of one year. The more we know about an individual, the more likely we are to develop that initial attraction that broadens by including friendship love, which is often the basis for a love that will last a lifetime. Married love is healthiest when it grows out of friendship. That's one of the purposes of dating—to give us opportunities to truly know the women we're going out with. Even after marriage, our wives want to know we are their friends as well as their husbands and lovers.

The New Testament was originally written in Greek, and in Greek there are three types of love: physical love, brotherly love, and the highest form of love, called *agape*. *Agape* is the way God loves us, and it's the type of love we strive to achieve with our wives. This love actively seeks to do the right thing for the other person. We want to meet the needs of our spouses, and *agape* means we willingly sacrifice our personal feelings and needs to meet the desires of our spouses. We willingly give up our rights and personal demands to seek to fill our partners' love tanks. This love moves beyond what we *feel* like doing; it patiently seeks to discover and meet the needs of our spouses regardless of the personal cost to us. We seek to rise above our humanness to meet the needs of our mates.

Our goal as Christians is to allow *agape* love to penetrate every relationship we have. To love this way, we must first know Jesus Christ as our personal Savior. Only through Him can we even hope to achieve a semblance of *agape.* We need to be submissive to His leadership and follow His principles. If we haven't made this basic commitment, we won't be able to enter into the realm of *agape.* Only through God's love, grace, and will are we able to enter into and experience this deeper type of love and allow it to permeate our relationships. *Agape* brings incredible depths of love and security to our marriages.

Gratitude All Day

Even though an earlier chapter focused on gratitude, I want to close with a challenge for you and me. Let's be deliberate in how we experience and express thanksgiving. It's so easy to take for granted all that we have, to fall into becoming more focused on worries than on wonder. Gratitude to God sets our hearts and minds on a clear and solid path. It's like sailors finding their true north so they can map the coordinates carefully and return home safely. Gratitude finds that focal point of God and allows us to gaze upon and glean from His grace, love, forgiveness, and guidance. Sometimes we need to consciously think and speak our gratitude so that it will become a routine attitude for our hearts.

For instance, do we wake up grateful for the chance to live another day, to serve God another day, to be with our families for another 24-hour adventure? If our first thoughts upon waking are less than jubilant, maybe we need to make a gratitude adjustment. In the early days of the Church of England, no songs were sung in English. The only exceptions were songs adapted from the book of Psalms. In 1674, a young pastor and school chaplain by the name of Thomas Kew wrote some English hymns for his young students. He encouraged these young men not to sing them in public—they were to be sung in their dorm rooms. These songs were prayers that he put to music. One prayer was for waking, another was for bedtime, and a third was for the midnight hour if sleep hadn't yet arrived. Here's his "awaking" song:

> Awake my soul and with the sun
> thy daily stage of duty run;
> shake off dull sloth and joyful rise,
> to pay thy morning sacrifice.

His evening hymn was:

> All praise to Thee, my God, this night, for all the
>   blessings of the light!
> Keep me, O keep me, King of Kings, beneath Thine
>   almighty wings.

These prayers turned into songs of praise and ended with a common stanza. This last stanza has since become the most widely sung verse in the world.

Praise God from whom all blessings flow;
Praise Him all creatures here below;
Praise Him above, ye heav'nly host;
Praise Father, Son, and Holy Ghost.[1]

Many churches and Christians haven't shared in the great encouragement of this stanza that has become such a popular part of our Christian heritage. If this isn't familiar, ask someone to sing it for you so you can learn it. You can also listen to it online. Singing this stanza will boost your spirits and renew your youthful sense wonder. If you start your day with gratitude, it's so much easier to keep on keeping on.

■■■ YOUR GUIDE TO LIVING YOUNG ■■■

Have you been looking down more than up? A shift toward optimism can be made when you replace worry with wonder. Do you remember what it felt like to go exploring as a young boy? I loved my childhood on our farm because I could always explore God's creation and the life cycle of the farm, the crops, the animals, and my family. It was a wonderful primer for the rest of my life. I learned many great life lessons, including the values of perseverance, patience, and hard work.

As you and I grow older, it's more important than ever to make space for God in our daily lives. I believe we can still experience the wonder and sense of adventure we had as boys, supplemented now with the wisdom and knowledge we've garnered through the years. Let's spend every day in God's presence. He is the only One who has known us since our mothers' wombs, and He is the One who will be with us forever. When we think in terms of forever, we are actually quite young!

1. What situation in your life feels like a marathon? How can you change your focus to motivate you to keep on keeping on with God?

2. When did you last laugh? Make it a point to laugh every day this week.

3. What makes you feel young?

4. Is there something from your childhood that helps you experience joy now?

5. What can you do this year that will bring joy to God, your family, and you?

PaPa Bob's Prayer

Dear God of Laughter, You've given me so many blessings and moments of great joy. I'm fortunate to look over my past years and recall so many times when I was surprised by Your provision and faithfulness. I'm grateful for Your healing love and Your guidance. Help me to have a thankful heart. Shape my first thoughts each morning so they focus on You. Where I encounter heartache or trouble, bring me into the comfort of Your presence and give me the strength I need to press on.

When I'm on my knees praying, praising, or pleading, Lord, set my thoughts on trusting You completely. Each day spent in Your presence is a glimpse of the joy that awaits me when I spend eternity with You. Fill my family with Your joy, God. Guide me to be a godly man who lives to serve You and the people around me with youthful passion and joy. Amen.

Notes

Chapter 2—A Good Man Loves Thanksgiving—Unless He's a Turkey

1. Adapted from *The Ryrie Study Bible*, New American Standard Translation (Chicago: Moody Press, 1978), Matthew 22:17, note 1485.

Chapter 3—Now's the Time for a Modeling Career

1. Ken Blanchard, *Inland Empire Business Quarterly*, Summer 1988, 25.

Chapter 4—I Married a Good Woman; She Married a Work-in-Progress

1. Alan Loy McGinnis, *The Friendship Factor* (Minneapolis: Augsburg Fortress Publishers, 52.

Chapter 6—Sometimes We Have to Lose Our Grip to Gain Our Balance

1. Denis Waitley, *The Seeds of Greatness Treasury* (New York: Pocket Books/ Simon Schuster Inc., 1983), 160.

Chapter 8—Even Old Bones Can Take a Leap of Faith

1. Adapted from Bob Barnes, *Five Minutes in the Bible for Men* (Eugene, OR: Harvest House Publishers, 2010), 91-93.

2. John Claypool, *Tracks of a Fellow Struggler* (Harrisburg, PA: Morehouse Publishing, 2004), 15-17.

3. Hope Lyda, *A Still and Quiet Place* (Eugene, OR: Harvest House Publishers, 2012), 21.

Chapter 9—Legacies Are Hand-Me-Downs People Actually Want

1. Stu Weber, *Locking Arms* (Sisters, OR: Multnomah Books, 1995), 50-51.

2. Leon Foster, ed., *6000 Sermon Illustrations* (Grand Rapids, MI: Baker Book House, 1992), 466, entry 4071.

3. Adapted from Emilie Barnes, *Meet Me Where I Am, Lord* (Eugene, OR: Harvest House Publishers, 2006), 131-32.

Chapter 11—Keep On Keeping On

1. Robert J. Morgan, ed., *Then Sings My Soul* (Nashville: Thomas Nelson Publishers, 2003), 20-21.

About the Author

Bob Barnes lives life to the fullest. Throughout his years of work in education, business, and ministry, he's enjoyed many opportunities to serve people. Retirement affords him more time to encourage his family, men, and the people who read his books. While this former farm boy is grateful for time spent working in the yard and garden, his favorite pastime is doing anything with Emilie, his partner in life and ministry. After more than 50 years of marriage, they enjoy one another's company while reading, going for walks, attending church and a small-group Bible study, and watching movies while sharing a bowl of popcorn. Together they inspire their kids, grandkids, and great-granddaughter by modeling a life of joy, commitment, and faith.

For more information about Bob and Emilie Barnes, their books, and their ministry, please send a self-addressed, stamped envelope to:

More Hours in My Day
2150 Whitestone Drive
Riverside, CA 92506
or write via email:
sheri@emiliebarnes.com